RECIPES FOR UNUSUAL GLUTEN FREE PASTA
Pierogis, Dumplings, Desserts and More!

RECIPES FOR UNUSUAL GLUTEN FREE PASTA
Pierogis, Dumplings, Desserts and More!

Danielle S. LeBlanc

La Venta West Inc.
Vancouver, Canada

La Venta West Inc.
Vancouver, Canada
www.laventawestpublishers.blogspot.com

Copyright © 2014 Danielle S. LeBlanc
Photographs copyright © 2014 Danielle S. LeBlanc
Paperback edition cover design by ilgeorgiev@fiverr.com
eBook cover design by cooking@fiverr.com

All rights reserved. No part of this book may be reproduced or utilized in any form or by any means, electronic or mechanical, including photocopying, recording, or by any information storage and retrieval system, without permission in writing from the publisher.

This book is intended as an informational guide. The recipes and techniques described herein are for educational purposes only, and not meant as a substitute for professional medical care or treatment. Please read the suggested contents of each recipe carefully and determine whether or not they may create a problem for you. We are not responsible for any hazards, loss or damage that may occur as a result of any recipe use or use of information provided herein. In the event of any doubt, please contact your medical advisor prior to use.

ISBN (eBook) 978-0-9920802-3-5
ISBN (paperback) 978-0-9920802-2-8

To my husband, Alex. Without him there would be no writing.

TABLE OF CONTENTS

Introduction 9

Chapter 1: Tools & Techniques 11
Chapter 2: Rolled, Sliced, and Diced Pasta... 17
Chapter 3: Noodle-Free Pasta & Grain-Free Noodle Alternatives..................... 27
Chapter 4: Stuffed Pasta - Wrapped, Boiled, Baked and Fried 39
Chapter 5: Fillings 51
Chapter 6: Sauces 59
Chapter 7: Some Not-So-Usual Soups, Salads, and Mains 67
Chapter 8: Beginnings and Endings - Breakfast and Dessert Pasta................. 79

Endnotes... 91
Index 93

Introduction

Most of us who can't have gluten miss pasta, and I'm not just talking about fettuccine, spaghetti, and spiral noodles. No, I'm talking about dumplings, won tons, ravioli, pierogi, orzo, couscous, and more. Believe it or not, all of these fall into the category of "pasta" as it has been defined by scholars of pasta-making history. Put simply, pasta is the end product of wheat or durum flour mixed with water or other liquids to create a kneaded dough which is cut into small shapes and then cooked in a moist environment (i.e. poached, boiled, or steamed).[i]

This loose definition of pasta blows open the proverbial cupboard door and allows all kinds of delicious dumplings, ravioli, and noodles to roll on out.

When I discovered in my late twenties that I was gluten intolerant, it took a while for the magnitude of what I would have to give up to sink in. I wasn't just losing bread and pizza. I was losing a massive chunk of my family heritage and the familiar foods of my youth. With one Polish grandfather and two German grandmothers, Polish pierogi, German spaetzle (egg noodles) and kartoffelklösse (potato dumplings) made regular appearances on family dinner plates.

I grew up with the smell of onions and pierogi sizzling in gobs of butter, and boiled potatoes waiting to be mashed, molded, and smothered with gravy. Living near a predominantly Polish / Ukrainian neighborhood of Winnipeg, Manitoba meant having restaurants specializing in homemade pierogi on almost every street corner. Competition for Winnipeg's best pierogi place was fierce.

Furthermore, the staff at the nearby Chinese restaurant worked in conjunction with my dad to teach me to use chopsticks before I was five. Around the same time, my mom learned to make won tons and my small fingers swiftly mastered the technique of folding the wrappers, helping to create dozens of delicious won tons to boil in homemade broth. Having to cut out gluten meant having to cut out most of the foods I'd grown up with such fond memories of.

However, over the years I've found ways to re-create some of my favourite family recipes. I've found that making gluten-free pasta doesn't have to be complicated and expensive, or require fancy equipment. All of the recipes in this book can be made using utensils most people already have, and the processes are explained in step-by-step instructions, often with pictures to guide you.

For centuries, people around the globe have been making pasta in some form or other in home kitchens using simple ingredients and techniques, and now you can, too. This book gathers together some of the more well-known forms of homemade pasta, along with delicious yet unusual, lesser known ones and some I've just made up in my quest to experiment with dough, fillings, and sauces. I hope you enjoy them as much as I do.

Recipes with a V indicate that the recipe is either vegetarian / vegan or has vegan options.

Chapter 1: Tools & Techniques

Making gluten free pasta doesn't have to be hard. It doesn't require expensive equipment or ingredients. It can be as simple as rolling out a sheet of dough, slicing it with a sharp knife, and boiling the pieces in a pot of water. However, knowing a few simple techniques, and the occasional use of specialized pasta making tools, can help expedite the process.

In this chapter:

Tools
Making a Steamer at Home

Rolling Fettuccine and Lasagna,
Making Ravioli

Tools

For centuries people have been making pasta in their kitchens using little more than a roller, a knife, and a pot to boil water in. That's still all you'll need to make most of the recipes in this book. However, there are some tools that, while not necessary, can make the process faster and easier if you choose to pursue pasta-making on a regular basis, or like to make big batches for freezing.

Sharp knife
Pizza cutter
Ultra-thin spatula or pie server
Pasta cutter
Ravioli maker
Ravioli stamp
Pierogi maker
Gnocchi board
Spaetzle Maker
Pasta Maker
Steamer

Making a Steamer at Home

Although commercial steamers, such as stackable bamboo steamers or plug-in devices, can be more efficient than a homemade steamer, they are not always practical for small kitchens or those just starting out with steaming. A homemade steamer can be made with a few simple utensils.

A large pot, such as a Dutch oven or canner
Tight fitting lid for pot
Pie plate or 8x8" square baking dish to fit inside pot
A raised rack, such as a cooling rack that will fit inside the large pot
(I have used the overturned jar rack from my canner)
Oven mitts
Tongs (optional)

To make the steamer:

Fit the rack inside the large pot. Add enough water to fill pot just below top of rack (ideally about 1-2" of water). Do not cover the top of the rack with water. This is the steamer.

The pie plates or baking dishes will serve as the steaming trays. When adding and removing trays from the pot, wear oven mitts for safety and use tongs to assist if desired.

To steam items, bring water to a boil, fill tray with items for steaming and, using oven mitts, carefully place the tray on the rack. If plates fit appropriately, stack one on top of the other. Cover pot with lid and steam as directed in recipe.

Rolling Fettuccine, Lasagna, and Ravioli

Most of the dough recipes in the first chapter of this book can be used in a variety of ways, some of which are described in the following chapters. But the most basic of techniques, rolling out and cutting fettuccine, lasagna, and ravioli, are described here. These techniques don't require any tools other than a rolling pin and sharp knife. If using a pasta maker, follow the machine's instructions for rolling out dough.

Note that while gluten free pasta freezes well, it does not dry as well as glutinous pasta. Therefore, instructions for freezing only are provided.

Rolling out Fettuccine and Lasagna:

1. Choose a dough option and make according to directions. Divide into quarters, or smaller if desired.

2. Dust a flat surface and rolling pin with sweet rice flour, or other flour as recommended in dough recipe. A wooden or bamboo cutting board is ideal for this. Alternatively, dough can be rolled between two pieces of flour-dusted waxed paper or plastic wrap to prevent sticking.

Turn out a piece of dough on to floured surface. Keep remaining dough covered with a clean, damp tea towel or damp paper towel to prevent drying out.

3. Roll dough out nearly paper thin in a rectangle, frequently dusting the dough and rolling pin with flour and flipping dough over periodically to prevent sticking. To flip dough or unstick it from the surface, slide a very thin, sharp knife or spatula under the dough, sprinkle with flour and turn over. Sprinkle dough with more flour and continue rolling.

4. To cut fettuccine noodles, slide a sharp knife or spatula under the dough to loosen from surface. Using a sharp knife, pizza cutter, or pasta cutter, cut thin strips lengthwise. Slide a sharp knife or spatula under the noodles again to loosen and gently lift off the surface.

To cut lasagna noodles, cut strips approximately 9" long x 2¼" wide.

Save dough scraps. To rework the scraps, knead a few drops of water into dough to moisten, then roll as directed.

5. Noodles can be dropped immediately into boiling salted water with approximately ½Tbsp olive oil and boiled for 1-2 minutes, until cooked through and floating. Drain and serve.

Alternatively, 3-4 noodles can be wrapped around two fingers to create a rosette and set aside while continuing to roll the remaining dough.

To Freeze Fettuccine: Slide a sharp knife under 3-4 strands of fettuccine. Wrap ends around two fingers, rolling dough over itself to create a rosette-like shape, as pictured. Place rolled dough on a baking sheet covered with waxed or parchment paper. Repeat with remaining dough, placing on sheet so rolls do not touch. Freeze for ½ hour, then transfer to a container with a tight-fitting lid. Separate layers of dough with waxed or parchment paper so they do not stick together. Freeze up to two months.

To Freeze Lasagna: Lay lasagna noodles out flat on a baking sheet covered with waxed paper or parchment paper. Freeze ½ hour, then transfer to a container with a tight fitting lid. Freeze up to two months.

To Cook: Remove fettuccine or lasagna from freezer and let thaw 5 minutes. Cook as for fresh noodles.

Rolled dough for freezing

Making Ravioli:

Ravioli can be cut a few different ways, depending on preference and equipment, but the below instructions call for no more than a sharp knife and rolling pin. It's as simple as rolling out a sheet of dough and dropping spoonfuls of filling at regular intervals, which are then covered with another sheet and cut into squares.

Pasta makers and accessories, which can make ravioli more quickly, are usually self-explanatory and come with instructions.

1. Choose a dough option and make according to directions. Divide into quarters, or smaller if desired. Keep dough covered with a clean, damp tea towel or damp paper towel to prevent drying out.

2. Turn one piece of dough out on to a smooth surface dusted with sweet rice flour. A wooden or bamboo cutting board is ideal for this. Alternatively, dough can be rolled between two pieces of flour-dusted waxed paper or plastic wrap to prevent sticking.

Frequently dust the dough and rolling pin with sweet rice flour, flipping dough over periodically to prevent sticking. To flip dough or unstick it from the surface, slide a very thin, sharp knife or spatula under the dough, sprinkle with flour and turn over. Sprinkle dough with more flour and continue rolling.

3. To shape ravioli, slide a sharp knife or spatula under the dough to loosen from surface. Very lightly brush surface of dough with water to moisten. Place ½ - ¾ tsp filling of choice approximately 1 ½" apart. Place a second sheet of dough overtop and press down around mounds of filling to avoid air bubbles. Using a sharp knife, pizza cutter, or pasta cutter, cut out squares around the filling. Press edges to ensure dough is sealed around filling.

4. Ravioli can be dropped immediately into boiling salted water and boiled until the ravioli float, then boiled an additional 1-2 minutes. Drain and serve.

To freeze: Place uncooked ravioli at close intervals (not touching) on a baking sheet covered in waxed or parchment paper and freeze ½ - 1 hour. Keep in freezer in tightly sealed containers up to one month. To cook, drop directly into boiling water and boil until ravioli float, then boil an additional 1-2 minutes.

Chapter 2: Rolled, Sliced, and Diced Pasta

Most pasta, whether it is fettuccine, ravioli, Turkish piruhi, orzo, or others, requires a good dough base to work from. The recipes in this chapter provide the starting point for making a wide variety of pastas, including many of the recipes in subsequent chapters, such as ravioli, *Turkish Piruhi*, *Beet Fettuccine*, and *Chow Fun*, and all have vegan options.

Shown below: Hand Cut Orzo

Basic Gluten Free Pasta Dough (with variations and vegan option)
Millet Flour Dough – vegan & gum-free
Steamed Rice Noodles (Ho Fun) - V
Hand-cut Orzo - V

German Spaetzle / Spätzle - V
Beet Pasta Dough - V
Pumpkin Pie Dough - V

Basic Pasta Dough (with variations and vegan option)

A basic dough that can be used for fettuccine, ravioli, pierogi, orzo, and more. It also serves as a base for fun variations such as *Chocolate Pasta Dough* and *Pumpkin Pie Spiced Dough*, described in later chapters. The sorghum flour version is particularly nutritious, while the white rice flour version is perfect for making brightly colored dough like *Tri Color Tortellini* and *Beet Fettuccine Dough*. Sweet rice flour, also known as glutinous rice flour for its glutinous texture (although it *is* gluten free), provides the slightly slippery texture common to pasta, while xanthan or guar gum helps bind the flours and prevents crumbling. Guar gum can be substituted for xanthan.

Serves 2-4

Sorghum Flour Dough

¾ c sorghum flour

2 Tbsp sweet rice flour + extra for dusting and rolling

¼ c tapioca starch

¾ tsp xanthan gum or guar gum

Pinch of salt

1 egg

1 Tbsp olive oil

Water by the spoonful (approx. 3-4 Tbsp)

1/16 tsp nutmeg (optional)

1. Sift together the flours, starch, gum, and salt into a large bowl. Create a well in the center of the mix.

2. Place the egg in the center of the well, along with olive oil and 2 Tbsp of water. Whisk together wet ingredients with a fork, then blend in dry ingredients, adding in water by the spoonful as needed until dough forms a ball. Dough should be smooth, but not overly sticky. If too sticky, a small amount of rice flour may be worked in during the process of rolling out dough.

3. Cover bowl with a clean, damp tea towel until ready for use. Dough can be refrigerated up to 24 hours before use, no longer.

Variations

* **Egg-Free or Vegan Pasta Dough:** Replace egg with 1 Tbsp ground flax mixed with 3 Tbsp warm water. Let mixture sit 5 minutes then mix into dough in place of egg. Egg-free version will be slightly less elastic than the egg version.

* **White Rice Flour Dough**: Replace sorghum flour with white rice flour.

* **Red Tomato Dough**: Use either sorghum or white rice flour dough base, minus the water, to create a crumbly mix. Add in 3 tablespoons plain tomato paste, and water by the spoonful while mixing to create a smooth, red dough.

* **Green Spinach Dough**: Make a batch of white rice flour dough, minus the water, to create a crumbly mix. Using ¾ c tightly packed spinach, wash and blanch the spinach in boiling water for 2 minutes, until wilted. Drain well, cool, and finely chop. Blend the spinach into the mix and add water by the spoonful to create a smooth green dough.

Millet Flour Pasta Dough - vegan and gum-free

Some of the world's oldest pasta was made from millet flour, as evidenced by a 4,000 year-old bowl of pasta made from millet flour found in China recently.[ii] While sweet rice flour, xanthan and guar gum help provide a texture close to regular, wheat-based pasta, not everyone can stomach rice flour and gum. This millet flour variation has a mild, nutty flavor and a somewhat chewy texture. The dough is moister than other variations and somewhat fragile until it's been boiled, so handle it gently. Millet flour pasta works well for thick cut fettuccine and lasagna noodles.

Serves 2-4

¾ c fine millet flour + more for dusting

¼ c tapioca starch

½ tsp salt

2 Tbsp ground flax seeds (a.k.a. flax seed meal)

6 ½ Tbsp warm water, divided

1 Tbsp olive oil

---

1. In a small bowl, mix together ground flax seed and 6 tablespoons water. Let rest 5 minutes.

2. In a medium-sized bowl, sift together millet flour, tapioca starch, and salt. Make a well in the center and add in flax seed mix, ½ Tbsp water, and olive oil. Blend in dry ingredients to create a smooth dough.

To roll out, dust a flat surface and rolling pin with millet flour. Divide dough in quarters and cover with a damp tea towel. Roll out one piece of dough, dusting regularly with flour and occasionally turning over.

To turn over, dust with flour, slide a long, thin, sharp knife under dough, lift and turn over. Dust top with more flour and continue rolling.

Slice dough into desired shapes, such as fettuccine or lasagna, with a sharp knife, pasta roller, or pizza cutter.

Steamed Rice Noodles (Ho Fun) - V

Commonly served as rolls for dim sum, or made into *Chow Fun*, a noodle stir fry, these easy gluten free noodles can make for a satisfying first foray into noodle making. They require a little bit of time to make, but require few ingredients or practiced skill. Using stackable steamer trays, or preparing one tray while another steams, can help speed up the process. See **Setting up a Steamer** for suggestions for creating your own steamer from common kitchen utensils.

Serves 4

1½ c white rice flour

½ c tapioca starch

1 tsp salt

2 c water

Neutral flavored oil for brushing

6 stalks green onions, finely diced (optional)

½ c dried shrimp (optional)

---

1. Whisk together flour, starch, salt and water.

2. Using a pastry brush, brush steamer trays with oil. Pour a thin layer of batter over each tray, enough to cover the bottom (i.e. approximately ¼ - ½ cup is needed to cover a 9" pie plate).

3. Sprinkle with optional green onions and/or dried shrimp if desired.

4. Place tray(s) in steamer and cover. Steam 4-5 minutes, until batter is nearly translucent and firm, yet flexible. Remove from steamer with kitchen mitts or tongs.

5. Brush top of noodle sheet with oil. Run an oiled spatula around the edges of the noodle, then work the spatula under the sheet.

From here the noodles can be either removed from the tray in one flat sheet (to be cut into noodle strips later) or rolled.

* **To remove whole noodle sheet:** gently work spatula under the noodle sheet, peel out of tray, and stack on top of one another to be cut into strips for *Chow Fun*, stir fries, or soup.

* **To make a roll:** work the spatula under the edge of the noodle sheet furthest away. Lift up the edge approximately 1" and fold it over. Continue working the spatula under the noodle sheet and rolling.

Brush used tray with more oil and repeat steaming process. Continue until all the batter is used up.

Serve rolls with gluten free soy sauce or Coconut Aminos (a gluten *and* soy free soy sauce alternative), or with *Asian Dipping Sauce*.

* **Tips -** Prepare a "work station" as follows to expedite the steaming process:

Keep a cooling rack near the steamer to rest freshly steamed trays on.

Keep a plate nearby for stacking noodle sheets or rolls.

Keep tongs or oven mitts handy to remove trays from steamer.

Keep a small bowl with oil nearby to dip brush in to.

Hand-cut Orzo – V

Orzo is often mistaken for a grain due to its small shape, which looks very much like grains of rice or barley. It is even known by some as egg-barley because of its shape, and the literal translation of the Italian word "orzo" means barley. However, orzo pasta is actually just finely chopped pasta dough, and to make it is a simple matter of technique. It can be served boiled and covered in sauce, in chilled salad, or in soup, as in *Orzo and Chickpea Soup*.

Serves 2-4

---

1 batch *Basic Gluten Free Pasta Dough* of choice

Sweet rice flour for dusting

1. Divide dough into sixteen equal portions. Turn one portion on to a flat surface dusted with sweet rice flour. Reserve remaining pieces in a bowl covered with a clean damp tea towel or paper towel.

2. Roll the dough against the flat surface to create a long, thin rope, approximately ¼" in diameter. With a sharp knife, slice into pieces ⅛" wide. The knife's pressure will press the dough down to create rice-shaped pieces.

3. To cook, bring a medium-sized pot of water to a boil, sprinkle with salt and 1 tsp olive oil. Add orzo and boil 1-2 minutes, until orzo floats.

Serve with one of the sauces in the *Sauces* chapter, or in *Orzo and Chickpea Soup*.

To freeze: Orzo can be spread out on a baking sheet covered with waxed paper and frozen for 30 minutes – 1 hour. Remove to a container with a tight-fitting lid and store in freezer up to one month.

German Spaetzle / Spätzle – V

Spaetzle is a type of pasta common in Germany and the surrounding countries. Its name translates as "little sparrow", which describes its tiny shape. Although spaetzle is not entirely unlike orzo in its size, the dough used to make it is thinner, and it is easier to use a tool, such as a spaetzle maker, colander, or potato ricer, to help shape the little drops of pasta.

There are a number of ways to serve spaetzle depending on preference and region of origin. My German Omi often served them one of three ways: fried in butter and sprinkled with nutmeg, with sauerkraut on top, or fried then smothered in cheese and gravy, almost like a German poutine! Nowadays I generally serve it with *Vegan Gravy*, sautéed greens, or covered in *Polish Cabbage and Mushroom Filling*.

Serves 2-4

---

1 c + 1 Tbsp brown rice flour OR sorghum flour

¾ c tapioca starch

1 ½ tsp xanthan gum or guar gum

¾ tsp nutmeg

½ tsp salt

2 eggs, beaten (or 2 Tbsp ground flax mixed with 6 Tbsp water for vegan option)

¼ c milk (use rice or almond milk for a vegan option)

Water by the spoonful as needed

1 Tbsp neutral flavored oil

Salt

1. Sift dry ingredients together. Mix in the 2 eggs, or flax eggs, and milk, mixing with a fork until the paste is able to form ribbons. Add more water by the spoonful as needed. The dough should be thinner than bread dough, but thicker than pancake batter.

2. Bring a few inches worth of water to a boil in a large pot and add 1 Tbsp oil and a few shakes of salt.

There are a few ways to add the spaetzle to the water:

a) Use a spaetzle cutter

b) Place a large-holed colander over the pot of water and, using a spatula, press the batter through the holes in to the boiling water – do this in batches, or work quickly as the batter on the bottom of the hot colander will start to cook onto the colander.

c) Add about 1/3 of the batter on to a cutting board and, using a knife or spatula, slide thin ribbons of batter off the board in to the boiling water.

3. Boil for approximately 2-3 minutes, until all the batter floats. Strain with a slotted spoon or hand held strainer and mix with a small amount of butter or oil to prevent sticking.

Sprinkle with salt and nutmeg or brown sugar if desired, or serve with one of the options in the description.

Alternatively, after boiling, spaetzle can also be fried in a pan with butter or butter substitute until lightly browned.

Beet Pasta Dough - V

Beet pasta dough is a fun way to impress guests with pasta that looks gourmet. It has a slightly earthy flavor that pairs well with *Olive Oil and Balsamic Vinegar Sauce, Browned Butter Sage Sauce,* or *Butter and Poppy Seed Sauce* and can be used for orzo, ravioli, pierogi, or fettuccine, as in *Beet Fettuccine*.

Serves 2-4

- ¾ c white rice flour, sorghum flour, or millet flour
- ¼ c tapioca starch
- ¼ c sweet rice flour
- ¾ tsp xanthan gum or guar gum
- ½ tsp salt
- 1 egg (or 1 Tbsp ground flax mixed with 3 Tbsp water)
- ⅓ c beet purée*
- 1 Tbsp olive oil
- 2-3 Tbsp water, as needed

1. Sift flours, starch, gum and salt together in a small bowl.

2. In a food processor, pulse egg, beet purée, and olive oil until smooth. Add in flour mix and pulse until blended. Add in water by the spoonful and continue pulsing until dough forms a smooth ball.

* To make beet purée, wrap 1-2 medium sized beets in aluminum foil and bake in a 425F oven for approximately 45 minutes, until soft. Cool, peel, chop, and purée in a food processor until smooth. Approximately ½ c chopped beets will make ⅓ c purée.

Pumpkin Pie Dough - V

Pumpkin Pie pasta dough can be used on its own, sliced as fettuccine and served with *Butter and Poppy Seed Sauce,* or made into ravioli and stuffed with *Sweet Potato Maple Filling,* or *Squash and Spinach Ravioli Filling* or dessert fillings, like *Pumpkin Pie Filling.*

Serves 2-4 as fettuccine, or enough to make 40-45 ravioli or pierogi

- ¾ white rice or sorghum flour
- ¼ sweet rice flour
- ¼ c tapioca starch
- ½ tsp xanthan gum or guar gum
- ¼ tsp salt
- ½ tsp cinnamon
- ⅛ tsp nutmeg
- 1 egg (or 1 Tbsp ground flax mixed with 3 Tbsp water)
- ¼ c unsweetened pumpkin purée
- 2-4 Tbsp water, as needed

1. In a medium-sized bowl, sift together flours, starch, xanthan gum, salt, cinnamon, and nutmeg. Stir to blend. Make a well in the center of the flours and add in egg or flax substitute, pumpkin purée, and 1 Tbsp water. Whisk egg and wet ingredients together, then blend in flours, adding water as needed until dough forms a smooth ball.

Refrigerate up to 24 hours before use.

Shown below: Ravioli with Squash and Spinach Filling topped with Browned Butter Sage Sauce and fresh chopped parsley

Shown below: Red Tomato Dough, Green Spinach Dough, and White Rice Flour Dough used to make Tri Color Tortellini

Chapter 3: Noodle-Free Pasta & Grain-Free Noodle Alternatives

Pasta is more than just noodles and ravioli. Gnocchi, *Ravioli Nudi, Kopytka,* and dough-free vegetable "noodles" all classify as pasta thanks to their flexible texture and cooking methods. Sometimes people with gluten issues have to get creative to mimic the texture, size, and flavor of regular pasta, so this chapter also offers healthy, grain-free alternatives to traditional wheat-based pasta noodles.

Shown below: Polish Kopytka

Gnocchi – V
Festival Squash Gnocchi – V
Kopytka, *kapytki* **("little hooves")**
Ravioli Nudi

Spaghetti Squash Pasta – V
Raw Zucchini Spaghetti / Fettuccine – V
Raw Sweet Potato Noodles – V
Mock Couscous - V

Gnocchi - V

Gnocchi are a classic Italian potato and flour based pasta. They are fluffy, yet sturdy and can be served with a variety of sauces, such as *Tomato Sauce, Basil Kale Pesto,* or *Tomato Cream Sauce.*

Makes approximately 130 pieces

3 lbs russet potatoes
¾ c white rice flour
¼ c tapioca or potato starch
¼ c sweet rice flour + more for dusting
½ tsp salt
⅛ tsp nutmeg
¼ c milk of choice (cow, rice, or almond, etc.)

1. In a large pot of boiling water, boil potatoes in their skins for 30-45 minutes, until soft. Remove from water and cool until able to handle. Remove skins and run through a potato ricer or mash until sm1. In a large pot of boiling water, boil potatoes in their skins for 30-45 minutes, until soft. Remove from water and cool until able to handle. Remove skins and run through a potato ricer or mash until smooth.

2. Mix flours, starch, salt, and nutmeg with potatoes, then mix in milk until dough forms a slightly sticky ball.

3. To form gnocchi, break off a chunk of dough. Cover remaining dough with a clean tea towel or paper towel. On a flat surface dusted with sweet rice flour, roll the dough into a long tube, approximately 1" in diameter. With a sharp knife, slice dough into ½" pieces.

*Gnocchi can be shaped in one of four ways:

a) With a fork, press down gently on each piece of dough to flatten and create indentation.

b) Roll dough pieces over a fork to create a cylindrical shape with fork indentation.

c) Press half way down on each piece of dough with a thumb to create a well.

d) Roll pieces over a gnocchi board to create uniform indentations.

To freeze: Arrange fresh, uncooked gnocchi on a baking sheet covered with waxed paper so they do not touch. Freeze 30 minutes – 1 hour, then remove to a container with a tight-fitting lid and store in freezer up to one month.

To cook: Drop gnocchi in a pot of boiling water with a pinch of salt. Cook in batches, and do not overcrowd the pot. When gnocchi floats, continue to cook 1-2 minutes. Remove with a slotted spoon.

Serve with one of the sauces from the *Sauces* section. Frozen gnocchi can be dropped directly in to boiling water, and may require an extra 1-3 minutes to float to surface.

Festival Squash Gnocchi - V

A lighter, less starchy version of traditional potato gnocchi, squash gnocchi makes a brightly colored dish. While this recipe calls for festival squash, a.k.a. carnival squash, a type of fall/winter squash, other similar types of squash like butternut or acorn can be substituted instead.

Makes approximately 90 pieces

1¼ c mashed or riced festival squash

(i.e. 1 small festival squash, sliced in half lengthwise and baked 30-45 minutes at 375F until soft, then peeled and mashed)

¼ tsp salt

⅛ tsp pepper

⅛ tsp ground nutmeg

¾ c white rice flour

¼ c sweet rice flour + extra for dusting

¼ c tapioca or potato starch

1. Mix squash, salt, pepper, and nutmeg together. Add in flours and starch and blend until dough forms a ball.

2. Divide dough into four pieces. Keep covered with a clean tea towel or paper towel.

3. Turn one piece of dough out on a flat surface dusted with sweet rice flour. Work in enough sweet rice flour to create a workable dough (about 1 Tbsp). Roll the dough into a long tube, approximately 1" in diameter. With a sharp knife, slice dough into ½" pieces.

***Gnocchi can be shaped in one of four ways:**

a) With a fork, press down gently on each piece of dough to flatten and create indentation.

b) Roll dough pieces over fork to create a cylindrical shape with fork indentation.

c) Press half way down on each piece of dough with a thumb to create a well.

d) Roll pieces over a gnocchi board to create uniform indentations.

To freeze: Arrange fresh, uncooked gnocchi on a baking sheet covered with waxed paper so they do not touch. Freeze 30 minutes – 1 hour, then remove to a container with a tight-fitting lid and store in freezer up to one month.

To cook: Drop gnocchi in a pot of boiling water with a pinch of salt. Cook in batches, and do not overcrowd the pot. When gnocchi floats, continue to cook 1-2 minutes. Remove with a slotted spoon.

Serve with one of the sauces from the *Sauces* section. Frozen gnocchi can be dropped directly in to boiling water, and may require an extra 1-3 minutes to float to surface.

Danielle S. LeBlanc ❖ Noodle-Free Pasta

Kopytka, *kapytki* ("little hooves")

Italians don't have the monopoly on fluffy, boiled, potato-based dough, although their gnocchi may be the most widely known form of potato pasta. Boiled potatoes and flour dumplings have been used around the world as a budget friendly way to feed large families, and for many it's a common comfort food. Unlike gnocchi, the potatoes in this Polish version are peeled prior to boiling, and an egg makes them extra fluffy. Their name, *kopytka*, or little hooves, comes from their shape which is like little deer hooves.

Makes approximately 100 pieces

---

3 lbs russet potatoes, peeled and quartered*

¾ c white rice flour

¼ c tapioca or potato starch

¼ c sweet rice flour + more for dusting

1½ tsp salt, divided

1 egg

---

1. Boil potatoes in a large pot of water with 1 teaspoon salt for approximately 30 minutes, until soft. Remove from water and cool.

2. Run potatoes through a ricer, or mash with a fork or potato masher, or pulse in a food processor approximately 15-30 seconds until smooth. Avoid over-mixing or potatoes will take on an undesirable texture.

3. Add rice flour, starch, salt, and egg. Mix with potatoes until a soft dough ball forms. If using a food processor, pulse until a ball forms.

To form kopytka: Break off a chunk of dough. Cover remaining dough with a clean tea towel or paper towel. On a flat surface dusted with sweet rice flour, roll the dough into a long tube, approximately 1½" in diameter. With a sharp knife, slice on a diagonal into ½ - ¾" pieces to create a hoof shape. Repeat with remaining dough.

To cook: Drop kopytka in a pot of boiling water with a pinch of salt. Cook in batches, and do not overcrowd the pot. When kopytka floats, continue to cook 1-2 minutes. Remove with a slotted spoon.

Frozen kopytka can be dropped directly in to boiling water, and may require an extra 1-3 minutes to float to surface.

To freeze: Arrange fresh, uncooked kopytka on a baking sheet covered with waxed paper so they do not touch. Freeze 30 minutes – 1 hour, then remove to a container with a tight-fitting lid and store in freezer up to one month.

Top with: Sauce of choice from the *Sauces* chapter or:

½ onion fried in 2 Tbsp butter over medium-low heat for 10-15 minutes, until onions are crispy. Or serve with ¼ cup gluten free bread crumbs sautéed in 2 Tbsp butter until browned and crispy.

* Tip: To prevent browning of peeled potatoes prior to boiling, keep peeled potatoes in a bowl of cold water.

Ravioli Nudi

Historically, "ravioli" was a loose term that didn't always refer to the stuffed dough pockets that come to mind today when we hear the term.[iii] *Ravioli nudi* are a sort of lazy Italian ravioli that stem from the medieval period, in which the filling is boiled without the typical doughy pasta wrapper, hence their name, "naked ravioli." Ravioli nudi are more fragile than their wrapped counterparts, so don't over-boil or they will break apart. Handle gently with a slotted spoon and serve on a bed of sauce, or drizzled with butter and fresh chopped sage.

Makes approximately 22-24 ravioli

- 3 c loosely packed fresh greens (i.e. kale, spinach, or Swiss chard)
- ¾ c ricotta cheese
- ¼ c parmesan cheese
- 1 egg, beaten
- ¼ tsp salt
- Pinch of nutmeg
- Pinch of pepper
- White rice flour as needed

1. Bring a medium-sized pot of water to a boil. Blanch greens for 1 - 2 minutes, until bright green and completely wilted. Drain, and when cool enough to handle, finely chop greens.

2. Mix all ingredients together in a bowl, adding white rice flour as needed to make a workable paste (approximately 2 - 4 Tbsp).

3. On a flat surface dusted with rice flour, roll into balls slightly smaller than the size of a golf ball.

4. With a slotted spoon, gently ease balls into a pot of simmering, bubbling water (avoid a rolling boil, as this may cause the balls to break apart). When balls begin to float, boil another 1-2 minutes. Gently remove balls with a slotted spoon and serve.

To freeze: Place *uncooked* ravioli nudi on a baking sheet covered in waxed paper and freeze 30 minutes – 1 hour. Remove to a freezer-safe container with a tight fighting lid and freeze up to 1 month. To cook, remove balls from freezer and let thaw in fridge 1 hour. Boil as directed above.

Shown below: Ravioli Nudi with Tomato Cream Sauce and freshly shredded parmesan

Spaghetti Squash Pasta - V

Some of the simplest pastas are not technically pastas at all, at least not in the sense that they are made from flexible flour and water dough. Spaghetti squash is a naturally gluten free, healthy, low carbohydrate, and grain-free alternative to flour-based pasta dough. The baked squash flakes off in thin, vermicelli noodle-like strips with a mild flavor that pairs well with both tomato-based and cream sauces.

Serves 4

1 large spaghetti squash

1. Preheat oven to 375F.

2. Slice squash in half lengthwise with a large, sharp knife. Scoop out seeds and soft pulp.

3. Place squash cut side down in a baking dish. Add enough water to immerse the squash approximately ½". Bake 30-45 minutes, until soft and a fork easily pierces the flesh.

4. Remove from oven and cool until easy to handle. With a fork, scrape out threads of squash.

5. Top with sauce and serve.

Can be refrigerated up to 72 hours before use.

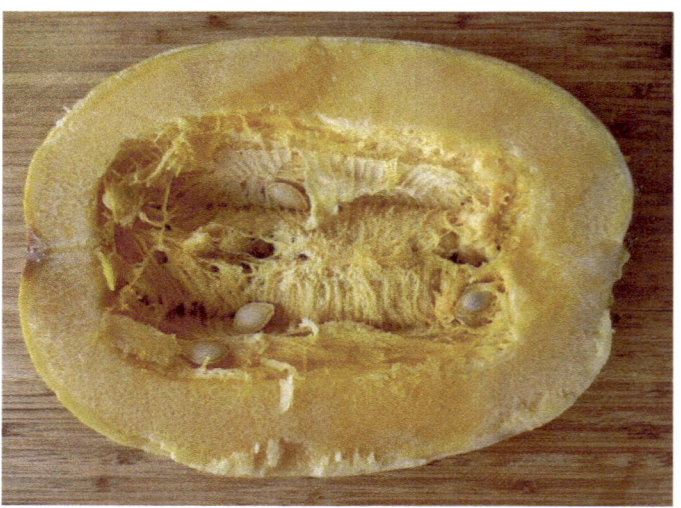

Raw Zucchini Spaghetti or Fettuccine Noodles - V

Like spaghetti squash, zucchini also makes a healthy, low carb substitute for flour based pasta dough. But unlike spaghetti squash, zucchini noodles are best served raw. Raw zucchini noodles make for a quick pasta on a hot day since they don't require standing over boiling water!

> There are a few different methods available for making noodles out of raw zucchini, such as a Spiral Vegetable Slicer, which create long, uniform spiral spaghetti noodles.
>
> Fettuccine noodles can be created by using a vegetable peeler to peel long strips of zucchini into ribbon-like strips. To create the noodles, turn the zucchini clockwise while peeling lengthwise down the stalk.
>
> Alternatively, a mandolin with a matchstick sized setting can be used to slice zucchini length-wise to create matchstick sized spaghetti noodles.

Raw Sweet Potato Noodles - V

Another quick and healthy grain free noodle option, Sweet Potato Noodles can be served raw or lightly sautéed.

> Sweet potato noodles can be made in the same way as zucchini noodles, using either a Spiral Vegetable Slicer, or a mandolin.
>
> Sweet potato noodles can be eaten raw, or sautéed in a small amount of olive oil, coconut oil, or butter substitute for 1-2 minutes, to soften slightly. Serve with sauce of choice.

Mock Couscous - V

Couscous, originally from North Africa, is made from semolina (derived from durum wheat) that has been rolled into tiny grain-like pellets. Over the centuries it has traveled the world and has been adapted to local cuisine. Israeli couscous, also known as *ptitim*, is similar to the North African style, but is slightly larger.

Both millet and quinoa grains make for nutritious and easy couscous alternatives. Both have a slightly nutty flavor. Millet makes for a sturdier final product, while quinoa is smaller and fluffier. Both work well with *Mock Moroccan Couscous*.

For Millet:
1 c dried millet (makes approximately 3½ c cooked)
2 c water or stock
¼ tsp salt

For Quinoa:
1 c dried quinoa (makes approximately 3 c cooked)
1 ¾ c water or stock
¼ tsp salt

For Millet:

1. Sift through millet and remove any dark pieces (these are usually just the un-hulled grains).

(Optional step) In a medium-sized, dry saucepan, toast millet over medium heat for 3-5 minutes, until golden brown, avoiding burning the grains. This helps to bring out the nutty, roasted flavor.

2. Add water or stock and salt to the millet in the pot, stir, and increase heat to bring water to a boil. Reduce heat to simmer, cover the pot with a tight-fitting lid. Simmer 15 minutes. Remove from heat and let sit, covered, for 10 minutes to absorb remaining liquid. Fluff with a fork and serve with desired sauce and/or vegetables.

3. Millet is best served warm. To reheat, add a small amount of water to millet and heat in a pot over low heat, or in the microwave in 30 second increments.

For Quinoa:

1. Rinse quinoa in a fine mesh strainer. This helps to remove the slightly bitter outer coating.

2. In a medium-sized saucepot, bring quinoa, water or stock, and optional salt to a boil. Reduce heat to low, cover with a tight fitting lid, and simmer for 15 minutes. Remove from heat and let sit, covered, 5 minutes to absorb water. Fluff with a fork and serve with desired sauce and/or vegetables.

Chapter 4: Stuffed Pasta - Wrapped, Boiled, Baked and Fried

Ravioli, pierogi, won tons, and dumplings are often out of reach for many with gluten issues. However, these can all be made at home as easily as making their glutinous counter-parts. Setting aside an hour (or employing friends and family) to make up a big batch of won tons, pierogi, ravioli, or dumplings can be a rewarding and satisfying experience.

Shown below: Tri Color Tortellini

Pierogi Dough & Shaping – V
Tri Color Tortellini – V
Won Tons - V

Steamed Dumpling Buns (Bao / Baozi) – V
Turkish Piruhi - V

Pierogi Dough and Shaping – V

Half-moon shaped Polish pierogi topped with sour cream, fried onions or sausage are certainly popular in North America, but in Central and Eastern Europe they go by several spelling and pronunciation variations, such as *pyrogy, pirogi, perogi,* etc., which all generally mean "pie". Pierogi are so popular that there's an old Polish expression linking them to a 13th century Polish monk. "Swiety Jacek z pierogami!" or "St. Hyacinth and his pierogi!" is roughly equivalent to saying "holy smokes!"[iv] Unfortunately the meaning of the saying isn't clear, but pierogi have clearly been around long enough to have a religious and even spiritual affiliation.

The most commonly known pierogi are stuffed with mashed potatoes and cheese. However, dinner pierogi can also be stuffed with sauerkraut, ground meat, or cabbage and mushrooms, or whatever leftovers happen to be in the fridge. Dessert pierogi are also served in Central and Eastern Europe, and can be stuffed with sweet fillings like jam, blueberries, ricotta cheese and fruit. Or, let your imagination run wild and fuse them with fun toppings like salsa or drizzled chocolate, and fill them with scrambled eggs and sausages.

Pierogi dough generally calls for a small amount of sour cream to provide a bit of tang, but if a dairy-free or egg-free, vegan option is desired, simply use one of the *Basic Pasta Dough* recipes from the front of the book.

Makes 40 – 45 pierogi

¼ c sorghum flour

½ c white rice flour

¼ c tapioca starch

¼ c sweet rice flour + more as needed for dusting

⅛ tsp salt

1 egg

3 Tbsp sour cream

1 Tbsp olive or coconut oil

1-2 Tbsp water, as needed

1. Sift together dry ingredients. Make a well in the center of the dry ingredients and add the egg, sour cream, oil and 1 Tbsp water. Whisk wet ingredients together with a fork, then blend in dry ingredients until smooth. Add water by the spoonful as needed until the dough forms a smooth ball. Dough should be smooth and not overly sticky. If too sticky, knead in a small amount of sweet rice flour when rolling out dough.

2. Divide dough into quarters, or eighths if desired. Turn one piece out on to a smooth surface dusted with sweet rice flour, such as a wooden or bamboo cutting board. Cover remaining pieces with a clean, damp tea towel or paper towel.

3. With a rolling pin, roll dough out nearly paper thin. To do this, frequently dust the dough and rolling pin with sweet rice flour, flipping dough over periodically to prevent sticking. To flip dough or unstick it from the surface, slide a very thin, sharp knife or spatula under the dough, sprinkle with flour and turn over. Sprinkle dough with more flour and continue rolling.

4. To shape pierogi, slide a sharp knife or spatula under the dough to loosen from surface. With a 2 ½" diameter round cutter, such as the rim of a glass or cookie cutter, cut out circles from the dough.

5. Place ½ - ¾ tsp filling of choice in the center of each circle. Slightly dampen a finger and run it around one half of the edge of the circle to moisten the dough. Fold the other half of the circle over the filling and pinch the edges together to seal. If desired, press down edges with a fork to seal and create indents.

From here, pierogi can be frozen or boiled immediately.

To freeze: Arrange pierogi on a baking sheet lined with waxed paper so they don't touch. Freeze 30 minutes – 1 hour, then move to a container with a tight-fitting lid. Freeze up to 1 month.

To boil: Drop pierogi into a large pot of boiling water. Do not overcrowd. When pierogi rise to the surface, continue boiling 2-3 minutes. Frozen pierogi may require an additional 2-3 minutes cooking time. Remove with a slotted spoon and serve.

If desired, after boiling, pierogi can be fried in a pan with 1 Tbsp butter, until browned and crispy on the outside.

*Tips: Prepare a "work station" with the following:

Sweet rice flour for dusting

A rolling pin

A small bowl of water

A baking sheet covered in waxed paper

Shown below: pierogi being shaped then fried in a skillet

Tri Color Tortellini – V

While packaged gluten free spaghetti, fettuccine, and lasagna noodles are making their way into most mainstream markets, gluten free tortellini can be hard to find. Like pierogi and ravioli, tortellini is simply stuffed pasta dough. It is the small belly button or turtle-like shape that makes it distinct. In fact, the word *tortelli* in Italian means "little cakes." In the European Middle Ages, stuffed dough pockets such as tortelli and ravioli were considered to be like bite-sized cakes, and so were sometimes fried like fritters instead of boiled.[v]

This recipe includes instructions for making the dough tri colored in beige, red, and green. However, a double batch of plain, *Basic Gluten Free Pasta Dough* can be used instead. Tortellini are easy enough to make and shape, but can be somewhat time consuming, so it helps to enlist a few extra hands to help. Luckily, though, tortellini freeze well and can be served with a variety of sauces, such as *Tomato Cream Sauce* or *White Cream Sauce*, or in *Spinach Tortellini Soup*. Stuff with filling of choice, such as *Ground Meat Filling*, or *Ricotta and Spinach Filling*.

Makes approximately 100 tortellini

1 ½ c white rice flour

½ c sweet rice flour + more for dusting

½ c tapioca starch

1 tsp xanthan gum or guar gum

½ tsp salt

2 eggs, beaten (or 2 Tbsp ground flax mixed with 6 Tbsp warm water)

1 Tbsp olive oil

2 ½ Tbsp tomato paste

2 oz spinach (approximately 2 handfuls of spinach)

Water by the spoonful, as needed

1. Blanch spinach in a pot of boiling water for 1-2 minutes, until wilted. Drain thoroughly and chop finely. Set aside.

2. Sift dry ingredients together and mix to blend.

3. Add eggs or flax mix and olive oil to dry ingredients and rub together by hand to create fine crumbs. Divide into 3 parts, approximately 1 cup each.

For plain colored tortellini: Adding water by the spoonful as needed (approximately 2 Tbsp) to 1 part of dough mix, blend until dough forms a smooth ball. Cover with a clean, damp towel or plastic wrap and refrigerate until ready to use.

For red colored tortellini: Add the 2 ½ Tbsp tomato paste and water by the spoonful as needed (approximately 2 Tbsp) to 1 part of the dough mix and blend until dough forms a smooth ball. Cover with a clean, damp towel or plastic wrap and refrigerate until ready to use.

For green tortellini: Add spinach, and water by the spoonful as needed (approximately 3 Tbsp) to 1 part of the dough mix and blend until dough forms a smooth ball. Cover with a clean, damp towel or plastic wrap and refrigerate until ready to use.

To shape:

1. Dust a flat surface with sweet rice flour. Divide each portion of dough into two. Roll out paper thin portions, dusting dough, surface, and rolling pin regularly with flour. Occasionally turn dough over by dusting with flour, running a long, thin knife under the dough, flipping over and dusting again. Cut out circles roughly 2" in diameter, using a cookie cutter, ravioli cutter, or the rim of a glass.

2. Place ½ tsp of filling of choice in the center of each circle. Dip a finger into a small bowl of water and lightly moisten one half of the circle's edge. Fold the circle over the filling to create a half-moon. Press edges together to seal.

3. Bring together the two pointed corners of the half-moon, dampen slightly with water, and press one edge on top of the other, sealing the corners to create a belly button or turtle-like shape. Repeat with remaining dough and filling.

To freeze: Arrange tortellini on a baking sheet lined with waxed paper or parchment paper. Freeze 30 minutes – 1 hour. Remove to a freezer-safe container with a tight fitting lid and freeze up to one month.

To boil: Bring a large pot of water to a boil. Drop tortellini into the water. When the tortellini begin to float, continue to boil a further 2-3 minutes. Frozen tortellini may require an extra 2-3 minutes to cook.

Unusual Gluten Free Pasta

Shown below: Tri Color Tortellini in Spinach Tortellini Soup

Won Tons – V

Most gluten intolerants mourn the loss of won tons, and, in particular, won ton soup. Rice paper makes an easy substitute for won ton wrappers, although they require the extra step of baking before boiling to prevent the wrappers from falling open. Bake them and serve them with *Asian Dipping Sauce* as finger food, or serve in *Won Ton Soup*. Rice paper can usually be found in the Asian section of most markets, in both square and circle shapes. The squares will be the easiest to wrap, but circles will work with a little adjustment.

Makes 24 won tons

6 sheets of square rice paper

2 cups filling such as *Asian Veggie Filling*, *Asian Shrimp Filling* or *Asian Meat Filling*

1. Fill a large bowl with warm water. Add one sheet of rice paper and let soak thirty seconds, until slightly softened. Remove from water and spread out on a flat surface. Using a pizza cutter or sharp knife, slice the rice paper into four equal sized pieces. These will be the won ton wrappers.

2. Scoop approximately 1 Tbsp of filling into the centre of one square. Fold one corner up and over filling. Fold opposite corner up and over, and repeat with remaining two sides, as if wrapping an envelope. Place on a baking sheet, with the side with the least amount of rice paper bulk facing upwards, and the side with all the folded paper down. Repeat for the rest of the fillings.

3. Bake in 350F oven for 10 minutes, until top is slightly firm and no longer tacky. Turn and bake another 5-7 minutes until the folded papers have sealed.

Steamed Dumpling Buns (Bao / Baozi) – V

Bao, or baozi, is a popular dish in Asian cuisine. This soft, slightly sweet yeast bread is like a cross between a bun and a dumpling thanks to the steaming process. The buns can be filled with a variety of fillings such as *Asian Veggie* and *Asian Ground Meat,* or sweet fillings like *Red Bean Paste* or sesame seed paste. Bao are known under various names, depending on the filling and the place of origin. The red bean paste dumpling buns shown in the photo below are commonly known as dousha bao, although they go by different names in different languages.

If a steamer is unavailable, one can be made with a few simple kitchen pots and pans (see *Creating a Steamer*). The buns take some time to make, but much of that time is spent waiting for the buns to rise. They're worth the wait!

Makes 10 buns

---

1 Tbsp active dry yeast

2 Tbsp + 1 tsp sugar, divided

½ c warm water

½ c brown rice flour

¼ c white rice flour+ extra for dusting

¾ c tapioca starch

½ tsp xanthan gum or guar gum

¾ tsp baking powder

½ tsp salt

Neutral flavored oil to coat dough

¾ - 1 c filling of choice

1. Proof yeast by mixing yeast, 1 tsp sugar and warm water in a small bowl. Let yeast rest no longer than 7 minutes.

2. Sift together the rice flours, starch, xanthan gum, baking powder and salt. Mix to blend. Blend yeast mixture into flours. Mix until a soft dough ball is formed.

3. Lightly grease a medium-sized bowl. Turn dough ball in bowl, flip dough over to coat completely. Cover with a clean dish towel and let rise in a warm place about 45 minutes, until nearly doubled in size.

4. Turn dough out on to a flat surface lightly dusted with white rice flour. Knead five or six times to smooth dough, then shape into a thick log. Slice into ten pieces.

5. Roll each piece into a ball, and then flatten using either a rolling pin or hands to create a circle approximately 3" in diameter. The center of the circle should be thicker than the edges, so that after shaping the dough will be evenly wrapped around the filling.

6. Place roughly ¾ - 1 Tbsp filling in the center of the circle. Working around the circle, pinch the edges of the circle together to wrap up around filling. Buns can be either left with the pinched edge upright, or rolled between the palms to create a smooth ball. 7. In a steaming dish place buns on squares of waxed paper. Steam in a steamer 8-10 minutes (see the section on *Creating a Steamer*), until buns are firm, yet slightly springy. Buns are best served warm.

Buns can be kept in the refrigerator up to two days and reheated in a microwave or steamer.

Unusual Gluten Free Pasta

Steamed Dumplings Buns with Red Bean Paste Filling

Turkish Piruhi – V

Turkish piruhi are actually very similar to pierogi or ravioli. They are simply two sheets of rolled out dough with spoonfuls of filling in between. The difference between the three, ultimately, is in the way that they are shaped, and the fillings commonly used. Ravioli is generally shaped into squares and stuffed with cheese or meat, while pierogi are half-moons typically stuffed with potatoes or sweet desserts. Turkish piruhi are somewhere in between, with a name that sounds close to pierogi, and the square shape and cheese filling of ravioli. However, a vegan filling such as *Artichoke and Spinach Filling* served with a topping of chopped nuts would also be suitable.

Makes 35-40 piruhi

---

1 batch *Basic Past Dough* of choice

Sweet rice flour for dusting

1 batch filling of choice (shown here with *Dill and Feta Filling*)

Pine nuts or walnuts for topping (optional)

Yogurt for topping (optional)

---

1. Divide dough into quarters, or smaller if desired. Keep dough covered with a damp tea towel or paper towel to prevent drying out.

2. Turn one piece out on to a cutting board or smooth surface dusted with sweet rice flour. Frequently dust the dough and rolling pin with sweet rice flour, flipping dough over periodically to prevent sticking. To flip dough or unstick it from the surface, slide a very thin, sharp knife or spatula under the dough, sprinkle with flour and turn over. Sprinkle dough with more flour and continue rolling.

3. To shape piruhi, slide a sharp knife or spatula under the dough to loosen from surface. Very lightly brush surface of dough with water to moisten. Place ½ - ¾ tsp filling of choice approximately 1 ½" apart. Place a second sheet of dough overtop and press down around mounds of filling to avoid air bubbles. Using a sharp knife, pizza cutter, or pasta cutter, cut out squares around the filling.

4. Piruhi can be dropped immediately into boiling salted water and boiled until the piruhi float, then boiled an additional 1-2 minutes. Drain and serve with yogurt and pine nuts, or as desired.

To freeze: *Place uncooked piruhi at close intervals (not touching) on a baking sheet covered in waxed or parchment paper and freeze ½ - 1 hour. Keep in freezer in tightly sealed containers up to one month. To cook, drop directly into boiling water and boil until piruhi float, then boil an additional 1-2 minutes.*

Shown below: Turkish Piruhi with Dill and Feta Filling and chopped cashews

Chapter 5: Fillings

For many home chefs over the centuries, stuffed pasta was a means of using up leftover bits of food, so don't just limit yourself to the fillings found here. Blanch some scraps of lettuce and blend them with diced olives and parsley, or finely chop leftover turkey dinner and mix it with mashed potatoes. Mix and match fillings with brightly colored dough to make a different type of pasta each week. A good rule of thumb to go by is that approximately 1 ½ cups of filling makes enough for about 35-50 ravioli or pierogi.

Shown below: Mediterranean Artichoke and Spinach Filling in Red Tomato Dough

Ricotta and Spinach
Dill and Feta
Squash and Spinach – V
Potato and Onion – V
Sweet Potato and Maple – V
Ground Turkey

Asian Ground Meat
Asian Shrimp
Asian Veggie – V
Polish Cabbage and Mushroom – V
Mediterranean Artichoke and Spinach – V

Ricotta and Spinach

Ricotta cheese and spinach is a simple, classic ravioli or piruhi filling that pairs well with most sauces.

Makes approximately 1 ½ c filling, enough for 40-45 ravioli or pierogi.

½ lb fresh spinach (or 1 package frozen spinach)
¾ c ricotta cheese
¼ tsp salt
½ Tbsp olive oil
¼ c grated parmesan cheese

1. If using fresh spinach, blanch 1-2 minutes in a pot of boiling water, until wilted. Drain thoroughly and cool until easy to handle. Finely chop spinach, or process in a food processor. Mix all ingredients together.

Can be refrigerated up to 48 hours before use.

Dill and Feta

Dill and feta make for a quick and simple filling for ravioli and piruhi.

Makes 35 – 40 piruhi or ravioli

½ c feta cheese (approximately 4-6 oz)
2 Tbsp freshly chopped dill

1. Mix together cheese and dill.

Can be refrigerated up to 48 hours before use.

Squash and Spinach - V

Healthy and veggie loaded, this filling pairs well with *Olive Oil and Balsamic Vinegar, Balsamic Browned Butter Sauce, Butter and Poppy Seed Sauce,* or *Browned Butter Sage Sauce*. Use with any variation of the *Basic Gluten Free Pasta Dough, Tomato Colored Ravioli Dough, Pumpkin Pie Dough,* or *Tortellini*.

Makes approximately 1 ½ c filling, or about 50 ravioli

- 2 Tbsp finely diced onion
- 1 Tbsp olive oil
- 3c chopped greens – i.e. spinach, kale, Swiss chard, etc
- 1 c mashed sweet squash, such as butternut or festival squash*
- ⅛ tsp nutmeg
- ¼ tsp dried basil
- Salt and pepper to taste

1. Sauté the onions in olive oil for 7-8 minutes, until translucent and just beginning to brown.
2. Add greens and sauté another 1-2 minutes until greens are wilted. Add nutmeg, basil, salt and pepper. Remove from heat, stir to mix and cool until easy to handle. Use as desired.

* To make mashed squash, slice a medium-sized squash lengthwise. In an oven-proof baking dish, place squash cut side down. Add enough water to ½" high. Bake squash in 425F oven for 30 minutes – 1 hour, until a fork slides easily into the squash. When cool enough to handle, scoop out seeds, peel and mash squash.

Can be refrigerated up to 48 hours before use.

Potato and Onion – V

A classic pierogi favorite, potato and onion filling is simple yet delicious. For a dairy-free option, use olive oil instead of butter, and cut out cheese, or substitute with dairy-free cheese.

Makes approximately 1 ¾ c filling, enough for 50 pierogi

- 1 ½ lb russet potatoes (approximately 1¾ c mashed potatoes)
- ½ medium-sized onion, finely diced
- 1 ½ Tbsp olive oil or butter
- ¼ c ricotta or shredded cheese (optional)
- ½ tsp salt
- ¼ tsp pepper

1. Peel and quarter potatoes. Bring a large pot of water to a boil and boil potatoes 30-45 minutes, until soft. Cool and mash with a potato masher, or run through a potato ricer.

2. Heat oil or butter in a large frying pan over medium heat. Sauté onions 7-10 minutes, until browned and slightly crispy.

3. Mix all ingredients together in a bowl.

Can be refrigerated up to 48 hours before use.

Sweet Potato Maple - V

A tasty filling for ravioli or pierogi.

Makes 1 ½ cups of filling, or approximately 35-40 pierogi or ravioli

- 1 ½ c mashed sweet potato*
- 1 ½ Tbsp maple syrup
- 3 Tbsp chopped parsley
- ⅛ tsp dried nutmeg
- ¼ tsp salt

1. Blend all ingredients together in a bowl.

* To make mashed sweet potato, bake 2 medium-sized sweet potatoes in an oven-safe dish at 375F for approximately 30 minutes, until a fork is easily inserted. Alternatively, cut sweet potatoes into halves and boil in a large pot of water for 15-20 minutes, until soft. Cool potatoes, peel, and mash with a fork or potato masher, or run through a potato ricer.

Can be refrigerated up to 48 hours before use.

Ground Turkey

Great for tortellini, ravioli, or piruhi, this filling can also be made with ground chicken, beef, or pork if desired.

Makes approximately 2 cups of filling, or roughly 75 ravioli

---

1 ½ c fresh greens, such as spinach, Swiss chard, or kale

2 Tbsp olive oil

½ small onion, finely diced

1 clove garlic, minced

1 lb ground turkey 1 large carrot, peeled and grated

2 Tbsp chopped fresh parsley

¼ c freshly grated parmesan cheese (optional)

1 egg

½ tsp salt

Pinch of black pepper

1. Bring a medium-sized pot of water to a boil. Blanch greens for 2 minutes, drain thoroughly and cool. Set aside.

2. In a large frying pan, heat oil over medium heat. Sauté onions for 5 – 7 minutes, until translucent. Add garlic and sauté 1 minute. Add ground meat and shredded carrot. Cook until meat is no longer pink, about 7 - 10 minutes. Remove from heat and cool 5 minutes.

3. In the bowl of a food processor, or with a sharp knife, add all ingredients together and finely process or chop until almost paste-like.

Keep refrigerated and use within 24 hours

Asian Ground Meat

This savory meat filling can be used in *Won Tons* and *Steamed Dumpling Buns*, and made with ground chicken, turkey, beef, or pork.

Makes approximately 1 ½ c

1 Tbsp olive oil

2" slice of fresh ginger, peeled and minced

1 clove garlic

½ lb ground meat such as chicken, turkey, or pork

2 c greens, such as spinach, kale, savoy cabbage, or Swiss chard

1 carrot, peeled and shredded

1 Tbsp gluten free soy sauce, or coconut aminos*

½ Tbsp rice vinegar

¼ tsp salt

Pinch of black pepper

1. In a large frying pan or wok, heat oil over medium heat. Add ginger and garlic and sauté 1 minute.

2. Add ground meat and sauté 7-10 minutes, until meat is cooked and no longer pink. Add greens, carrot, gluten free soy sauce, rice vinegar, salt and black pepper and sauté until greens and carrot are wilted.

3. Remove from heat and cool 5 minutes.

4. In the bowl of a food processor or, using a sharp knife, grind ingredients until almost paste-like.

Keep refrigerated and use within 24 hours

* Coconut aminos are both gluten and soy free. Always check ingredients before use to ensure gluten free status.

Asian Shrimp

This shrimp filling is great for *Won Tons* and *Steamed Dumpling Buns*.

Makes enough for 24 won tons

1 tsp minced ginger

¾ lb shrimp, peeled, deveined, and finely chopped

1 tsp sugar

2 water chestnuts, finely chopped

¼ tsp salt

½ Tbsp rice vinegar

2 tsp tapioca starch

Dash of pepper

1. Combine all ingredients in a bowl and toss to blend. Refrigerate before use.

Asian Veggie - V

This filling can be used for *Rice Paper Won tons* and *Steamed Dumpling Buns (Bao)*. Savoy cabbage is ideal, but plain green or red cabbage also work well.

Makes approximately 2 cups of filling

- 1 Tbsp oil for frying
- 1 garlic clove, finely minced
- 2" slice of fresh ginger, peeled and grated or finely minced
- 1½ cup shredded cabbage
- ¾ cup grated carrot
- 2 water chestnuts, finely diced
- 3 dried Chinese mushrooms (soaked in warm water for 20 minutes and finely minced)
- 2 Tbsp gluten free soy sauce or Coconut Aminos*
- ½ Tbsp rice vinegar

1. In a large skillet or wok over medium heat, heat oil and sauté the garlic and ginger for one minute to release the flavours.

2. Add cabbage, carrots, chestnuts, and mushrooms. Sauté for 5 minutes to soften.

3. Remove from heat and stir in the GF soy sauce of choice and rice vinegar.

4. Wait until filling is cool enough to handle before using to fill won tons or dumplings.

Can be refrigerated up to 48 hours before use.

* Coconut aminos are both gluten and soy free. Always check ingredients before use to ensure gluten free status

Polish Cabbage and Mushroom Filling - V

This cabbage and mushroom mix is a traditional Polish pierogi filling, and is great served with sour cream or sprinkled with brown sugar and cinnamon.

Makes approximately 1½ cups filling, or enough for 40-45 pierogi.

½ head of a large green cabbage, shredded (approximately 4 cups worth)

½ onion, finely diced

1 Tbsp olive oil or butter

2-3 oz canned mushrooms, finely chopped

¼ c water

½ tsp salt

⅛ tsp black pepper

1. Add all ingredients except salt and pepper to a medium – large sized sauce pot heated over medium heat.

2. Cook 5-7 minutes, until cabbage begins to collapse in size. Reduce heat to a simmer and cook until tender, stirring occasionally and adding water by the tablespoon as needed.

3. Remove from heat and drain. When cooled enough to handle, chop finely or pulse in a food processor. Add salt and pepper to taste.

Mediterranean Artichoke and Spinach - V

A light and healthy ravioli / pierogi filling, this Mediterranean fusion filling works well served with a mild dressing like *Olive Oil and Balsamic Vinegar*, or, for a richer flavor try *Browned Butter Sage Sauce* or *Balsamic Browned Butter Sauce*.

Makes approximately 1½ cups filling, or enough for 40-45 pierogi.

---

1. In the bowl of a food processor, pulse ingredients until finely chopped. Alternatively, finely chop artichoke hearts, parsley, and spinach with a sharp knife, then blend together with lemon juice, salt, pepper and cheese.

Can be refrigerated up to 48 hours before use.

1 – 7 oz can artichoke hearts, drained

4 Tbsp freshly chopped parsley

1 c tightly packed spinach, washed and dried

1 tsp lemon juice

¼ tsp salt

¼ tsp pepper

¼ c shredded parmesan cheese (optional)

Chapter 6: Sauces

Mix and match pastas and sauces to create a variety of dishes. Below, fresh *Orzo* is served with *Basil Kale Pesto / Pistou* and freshly shredded parmesan for a simple and easy meal.

Shown below: Pumpkin Pie Dough with Butter and Poppy Seed Sauce

Basil Kale Pesto / Pistou - V
Olive Oil and Balsamic Vinegar - V
Balsamic Browned Butter Sauce
Browned Butter Sage Sauce - V
Red Wine Tomato Sauce - V
5 Minute Tomato Sauce – V

Tomato Cream Sauce - V
Asian Dipping Sauce - V
Vegan Gravy
Butter and Poppy Seed Sauce - V
White Cream Sauce - V

Basil Kale Pesto / Pistou – V

Pesto or pistou? The difference is actually in the allergens. Pistou is essentially pesto, but without the nuts or cheese. This recipe can be customized to add or remove the nuts or cheese depending on your preference. Serve pesto and pistou plain over all kinds of pasta or mixed in with tomato sauce, or serve on pizza, flatbread, or toast. This version calls for an injection of kale, a healthy super food.

Makes approximately 1 cup

- 1 c loosely packed fresh basil leaves, stems removed
- 1 c chopped kale leaves, stems removed
- 2 cloves garlic
- ¼ c pine nuts (optional)
- ½ c pecorino or parmesan cheese (optional)
- 2 tsp lemon juice
- 1/3 c extra virgin olive oil
- Salt and pepper to taste

1. Add all ingredients except oil and salt and pepper into the bowl of a food processor. Pulse to blend, then slowly blend in oil while pulsing. Mix in salt and pepper to taste.

Pesto / pistou can be frozen up to 3 months in the freezer.

Olive Oil and Balsamic Vinegar – V

A simple, light sauce for vegetarian ravioli, such as *Mediterranean Artichoke and Spinach Filling*, or unusual fettuccine, such as the type made with *Beet Pasta Dough*.

Makes 7 tablespoons of sauce and serves 4

- 4 Tbsp extra virgin olive oil
- 2 ½ Tbsp balsamic vinegar
- 2 Tbsp chopped fresh parsley
- Salt to taste

1. Toss together all ingredients and drizzle over pasta.

Balsamic Browned Butter Sauce – V

A rich sauce with deep flavor, this balsamic browned butter sauce is heavenly served over ravioli and fettuccine.

Makes 5 tablespoons and serves 4

- 4 Tbsp butter (or dairy-free butter substitute)
- 2 Tbsp balsamic vinegar
- ½ tsp dried sage
- Salt and pepper to taste

1. In a large skillet over medium heat, heat the butter and cook until it just begins to brown.
2. Add balsamic vinegar. Heat 1 minute to blend flavors. Remove from heat, add sage, salt and pepper and drizzle over pasta.

Browned Butter Sage Sauce – V

Browned butter and sage is a simple, yet flavorful sauce that can be used for ravioli, piruhi, pierogi, and even fettuccine.

Makes enough for 2-4 servings

4 Tbsp butter (or dairy free butter substitute)

8-10 fresh sage leaves, roughly chopped

Salt and pepper to taste

½ Tbsp brown sugar (optional)

1. In a small saucepan, heat butter or alternatives over medium-low heat for 3-5 minutes, until browned.

2. Add sage leaves to pan and heat 1 minute, until leaves are wilted. Remove from heat, add salt, pepper, and sugar, if desired. Drizzle over pasta and serve.

Red Wine Tomato Sauce - V

Red wine adds a richness to pasta sauce that can't be beat. This sauce is simple, yet flavourful, and can be served over most types of fettuccine, ravioli, or gnocchi.

Serves 4-6

1. Blanch tomatoes in a pot of boiling water until the peel splits. Remove peel and roughly dice tomatoes.

2. In a medium-sized saucepot, heat oil over medium heat. Sauté onion and garlic 5-7 minutes, until onion is softened. Add red wine, diced tomatoes, olives, and herbs. Bring to a boil, then reduce to simmer for 20-25 minutes to reduce liquid. Add salt and pepper to taste.

2 large tomatoes, blanched in boiling water and peeled (or 1-15oz can diced tomatoes)

1 Tbsp oil

2 Tbsp finely diced onion

1 clove garlic

¼ c red wine

¼ c Kalamata olives, pits removed and thinly sliced

1 tsp dried or 1 Tbsp fresh oregano

1 tsp dried or 1 Tbsp fresh basil

Salt and pepper to taste

5 Minute Tomato Sauce - V

This quick and easy tomato sauce can be served cold over raw or cooked vegetable noodles like *Spaghetti Squash Pasta*, *Sweet Potato Noodles*, or *Raw Zucchini Spaghetti or Fettuccine*. Or heat the sauce in a saucepan to serve over freshly made *Fettuccine Noodles*, gnocchi, or ravioli.

Serves 4

> 1 - 15oz can diced tomatoes
> 1 Tbsp olive oil
> 1 clove garlic
> ¼ c gluten free vegetable stock
> ¼ bunch fresh parsley
> 1 tsp fish sauce (optional)
> 10 fresh basil leaves + extra for garnishing
> Salt and pepper to taste

1. In a blender, blend all ingredients until smooth. Serve cold or warm, with fresh basil and parmesan if desired.

Tomato Cream Sauce - V

Tomato Cream Sauce is a great topping for all kinds of pasta, such as plain fettuccine noodles, ravioli, *Ravioli Nudi*, vegetable noodles such as *Spaghetti Squash*, and raw zucchini.

Serves 4

> 2 Tbsp olive oil
> ½ medium-sized onion, finely diced
> 2 cloves garlic, minced
> 1 – 14.5 oz can diced tomatoes
> 1 Tbsp dried basil
> ½ tsp dried oregano
> ½ tsp salt
> ⅛ tsp black pepper
> ½ c heavy cream*
> 1 Tbsp butter or dairy free alternative
> 1 tsp brown sugar

1. In a medium-sized sauce pot, heat oil over medium heat. Add onion and sauté 5-7 minutes, until translucent. Add garlic and sauté another minute.

2. Add tomatoes and bring to a boil. Continue to boil 5 minutes, until some of the liquid evaporates. If a smooth sauce is desired, remove from heat and run through a blender or food processor.

3. Return to heat and stir in basil, oregano, salt, pepper, cream, and butter. Reduce heat and simmer 5 minutes. Remove from heat and serve.

* For a lighter and/or vegan version: Substitute milk or dairy-free milk such as rice or almond milk instead of cream.

Asian Dipping Sauce - V

Made with gluten free soy sauce, or Coconut Aminos for a gluten and soy free option, this dipping sauce is great for *Steamed Rice Noodle Rolls* and *Won Tons*.

Makes 2½ Tbsp sauce

- 1 Tbsp gluten free soy sauce or Coconut Aminos
- ½ Tbsp rice vinegar
- ½ Tbsp water
- ½ tsp minced ginger
- ¼ tsp sesame oil

1. Mix all ingredients together in a small bowl and serve.

Vegan Gravy

Served with spaetzle, gnocchi, kopytka, or other dumplings, gravy is a comforting topping and with this vegan version you won't even miss the meat.

Makes 2 ½ cups

- 2 Tbsp vegan butter or coconut oil
- ½ c white or button mushroom, chopped
- ½ onion, minced
- 3 Tbsp white rice flour
- ½ tsp dried thyme
- 2 c vegetable broth
- 1 bay leaf
- Salt and pepper to taste

1. In a large skillet, melt butter or coconut oil over medium heat. Add mushrooms and onion. Sauté 5 – 7 minutes to soften.

2. Add flour and thyme and stir to coat mushrooms and onions. Add broth and bay leaf, stirring to avoid lumps. Bring broth to a boil then reduce to simmer for 8-10 minutes to thicken, stirring frequently. Add salt and pepper to taste.

Shown below: White Cream Sauce with Spaghetti Squash Pasta, recipe on next page

Butter and Poppy Seed Sauce – V

Shown above with *Pumpkin Pie Dough*, this easy butter and poppy seed sauce pairs well with fettuccine and ravioli dishes.

Makes 4 tablespoons of sauce and serves 2-4

4 Tbsp butter (or dairy-free butter substitute)
1 Tbsp poppy seeds
4 fresh sage leaves, roughly chopped
1 tsp brown sugar

1. In a small sauce pan, melt butter over medium-low heat. Cook until butter begins to brown. Stir in poppy seeds and sage. Remove from heat, drizzle over pasta and sprinkle with brown sugar.

White Cream Sauce - V

Shown here with *Spaghetti Squash Pasta*, this white cream sauce goes well with fettuccine, spaghetti squash, *Sweet Potato Noodles*, and *Raw Zucchini Spaghetti or Fettuccine*.

Makes 1 ½ cups sauce and serves 4

1. In a heavy saucepan, heat butter or oil over medium heat. Add onion and garlic and sauté 7-8 minutes until translucent. Stir in flour to coat.

2. Add cream, broth and optional vegetables if using. Reduce heat to medium-low and simmer gently until sauce is thickened and vegetables are softened, about 8-10 minutes.

3. Whisk in herbs, simmer 5 minutes, add salt and pepper to taste and serve.

2 Tbsp butter or olive oil
2 cloves garlic, minced
1 small red onion, finely diced
1 Tbsp rice flour
1 c heavy cream
(or dairy free alternative, such as rice milk, almond milk or coconut milk)
½ c gluten free chicken or vegetable broth
¼ c chopped fresh parsley + extra for garnish
½ Tbsp chopped fresh sage
Salt and pepper to taste
<u>Optional</u>
½ zucchini, diced in ½" chunks
¼ c hulled peas
1 carrot, peeled and diced
½ c broccoli florets

Chapter 7: Some Not-So-Usual Soups, Salads, and Mains

Still looking for more ways to use up those won tons, orzo, beet fettuccine, tortellini, and couscous? Try some of these delicious meals and unusual soups, salads, and mains.

Shown below: Orzo and Chickpea Soup

Won Ton Soup - V
Mock Moroccan Couscous Tagine - V
Spinach Tortellini Soup - V
Orzo and Chickpea Soup - V

Chow Fun - V
Lemon Salmon Pasta
Beet Fettuccine - V
Vegan Lasagna

Won Ton Soup – V

Won Ton Soup makes a comforting appetizer or a light meal, whether the won tons are filled with *Asian Ground Meat Filling, Veggie Filling, or Shrimp Filling*. Once the *Won Tons* are prepared, this soup takes only a few minutes to make.

Serves 6

1 batch *Won Tons* with filling of choice, baked according to *Won Tons* directions

6 cups gluten free chicken or vegetable broth

1 Tbsp gluten free soy sauce or Coconut Aminos, plus more as desired

Salt and pepper

2 stalks green onions, finely diced

1. In a large sauce pot, heat broth over medium heat. Add won tons and simmer 5 minutes. Remove from heat and add soy sauce, and salt and pepper to taste. Serve garnished with diced green onions.

Mock Moroccan Couscous Tagine - V

Sometimes beautifully hand-painted, a tagine is a clay cooking pot with a conical-shaped lid commonly used in North Africa. "Tagine" can also refer to the type of dish cooked in a tagine pot, and recipes vary widely. The shape and clay base of a tagine keep food moist and the flavor rich. A traditional tagine pot is ideal for this lightly spiced Mock Moroccan Couscous, which substitutes quinoa for the regular glutinous couscous. However, a ceramic or glass baking dish may be used instead of a tagine.

Serves 4-6

½ c water or GF chicken or vegetable stock
½ tsp cumin
¼ tsp cinnamon
½ tsp paprika
¼ tsp turmeric
⅛ tsp red pepper flakes
½ tsp salt
¼ tsp black pepper

2 Tbsp olive oil
2 shallots, finely diced
2 cloves garlic, minced
1" slice of ginger, peeled and minced
2 carrots, peeled and chopped into ½" chunks
1 parsnip, peeled and chopped into ½" chunks
1 medium sized turnip, peeled and chopped into ½" chunks
1 medium-sized sweet potato, peeled and chopped into ½" chunks
¼ c raisins (optional)

1 c dry quinoa
2 c water or stock

Fresh chopped parsley for garnish

Preheat oven to 375F.

1. Whisk together water, cumin, cinnamon, paprika, turmeric, red pepper flakes, salt, and pepper. Set aside.

2. In a frying pan or tagine dish (following manufacturer's directions), heat oil over medium heat. Add diced shallots and fry 7-10 minutes, until beginning to brown, stirring occasionally. Add garlic and ginger and fry 1 minute.

3. Toss shallots, garlic, and ginger with the carrots, parsnip, turnip, sweet potato, and raisins (if using) in a baking dish or tagine. Pour over the water and spice mixture and toss. Place lid on tagine or cover baking dish with a tight-fitting lid or aluminum foil.

4. Roast tagine or baking dish in oven for 45 minutes, until vegetables are soft. Baste with spice mixture ½ way through.

5. While tagine is cooking, prepare quinoa. Rinse quinoa in a fine mesh sieve. In a medium-sized pot, bring quinoa and water or stock to a boil. Reduce heat to simmer and let cook, covered, 15 minutes. Remove from heat and let sit with lid on 5 minutes. Fluff with a fork.

Serve tagine spooned over quinoa and garnish with fresh parsley.

Spinach Tortellini Soup – V

This tortellini soup can be served as a delicious appetizer or a healthy meal in itself. Use a vegetable filling and eliminate the parmesan garnish for a vegan dish.

Serves 4

2 Tbsp olive oil

½ c finely diced onion

1 clove garlic, minced

1 carrot, peeled and sliced into thin rounds

½ zucchini, diced into ½" chunks

5 c chicken or vegetable stock

1 - 14oz can diced tomatoes

4 servings of *Tri Colored Tortellini* (approximately 28 tortellini)

⅛ - ¼ tsp red pepper flakes (depending on desired level of heat)

1 tsp dried oregano

½ tsp salt + more to taste

¼ tsp black pepper + more to taste

2 c loosely packed spinach, Swiss chard or kale leaves

Shredded parmesan and/or parsley for garnish (optional)

1. In a large pot, heat oil over medium heat. Add onion and garlic and sauté 7-8 minutes, until onion is translucent.

2. Add carrots, zucchini, stock, and canned tomatoes. Bring to a boil then reduce to simmer 10 minutes, until carrots are softened.

3. Add tortellini, red pepper flakes, and oregano. Simmer until tortellini float, then cook another 3-4 minutes.

4. Remove from heat, stir in spinach or other greens to wilt. Adjust salt and pepper to taste and serve with shredded parmesan and parsley to garnish.

Orzo and Chickpea Soup – V

One cup of fresh, *Hand-cut Orzo* from the *Rolled, Sliced, and Diced Pasta* chapter and some fresh vegetables make for a quick and hearty soup.

Serves 4

1 c fresh or frozen *Orzo* pieces
2 Tbsp olive oil
2 cloves garlic
½ medium-sized onion, finely diced

1 carrot, peeled and chopped into ½" chunks
1 - 15oz can stewed tomatoes
2 ½ c stock
1 - 15oz can chickpeas, drained
2 bay leaves
½ tsp salt
¼ tsp black pepper
¼ c chopped fresh parsley + extra for garnish
3 c loosely packed greens, such as chopped kale, spinach or Swiss chard leaves
Grated parmesan or dairy – free cheese to garnish (optional)

1. In a large saucepot, heat oil over medium heat. Add garlic and onion and sauté 5-7 minutes to soften.
2. Add carrot, tomatoes, stock, chickpeas, bay leaves, salt, pepper, and parsley and cook 15 minutes, until carrots are softened
3. Add orzo and greens. Cook 2 minutes, or until orzo is soft.
4. Serve garnished with parmesan cheese and parsley.

Chow Fun – V

Chow Fun refers to wide, stir-fried rice noodles, such as the ones in *Steamed Rice Noodles (Ho Fun)*, and is usually fried with meat, vegetables and sauce. Don't feel constrained by the ingredients in this recipe, though, as Chow Fun is flexible and can be made with leftover bits of chicken, beef, pork, shrimp, or vegetable odds and ends from the fridge.

Serves 4-6

1 batch *Steamed Rice Noodles (Ho Fun)*, or approximately 8 oz wide, flat rice noodles (such as Pad Thai noodles)
2 Tbsp oil for sautéing
1" piece ginger, peeled and minced
1 clove garlic, minced
¼ yellow onion, thinly sliced
2 carrots, peeled and thinly sliced in rounds
2 dried Asian mushrooms, soaked in hot water 20 minutes and finely chopped
2 c shredded green cabbage or sui choy
1 c broccoli
½ medium-sized zucchini, thinly sliced in rounds

Sauce
1 Tbsp brown sugar
1 tsp chili paste
1/3 c GF vegetable or chicken stock
3 Tbsp gluten free soy sauce or Coconut Aminos
2 Tbsp rice vinegar
1 tsp toasted sesame oil
2 tsp white rice flour or cornstarch
Salt to taste
¼ c chopped fresh cilantro to garnish

1. Prepare vegetables and set aside. Mix sauce ingredients together in a small bowl and set aside.

2. If using fresh *Steamed Rice Noodles*, slice rice noodle sheets into thick noodles, approximately ½" wide. If using packaged rice noodles, cook according to package directions until softened.

3. Heat oil over medium heat in a wok or large frying pan or pot. Add ginger and sauté 1 minute. Add garlic and onion and sauté 3-5 minutes to soften. Add vegetables and sauté 5-7 minutes to soften.

4. Add sauce and noodles and toss gently to coat. Serve garnished with cilantro.

Lemon Salmon Pasta

Baked salmon and cherry tomatoes laid out over pasta and greens, and then topped with lemon and capers.
Serves 4

For Baked Salmon:
½ Tbsp olive oil
½ Tbsp lemon juice
¼ tsp salt
Pinch of black pepper
1 lb wild salmon
½ pint grape or cherry tomatoes

For Pasta:
1 batch *Basic Pasta Dough* of choice, sliced into fettuccine noodles
(or 8 oz gluten free fettuccine noodles)
3 c loosely packed fresh greens, such as kale, spinach, or Swiss chard
1 clove garlic, minced
1 ½ Tbsp olive oil
1 ½ Tbsp lemon juice
¼ c chopped fresh basil leaves
3 Tbsp capers
Salt and pepper to taste

Shredded parmesan (optional)

Preheat oven to 400F.

1. Mix together oil, lemon juice, salt, and pepper. On a large sheet of aluminum foil, lay out salmon. Top with tomatoes and drizzle with lemon juice mixture. Wrap foil up over salmon and twist the top over itself to seal. Bake until salmon is cooked through and flakes apart with a fork, about 20-25 minutes.

2. Meanwhile, bring a large pot of salted water to a boil. If using fresh pasta, cook until noodles float and are tender (2-3 minutes). If using packaged noodles, prepare according to package directions. Drain noodles and return to pot. Add greens to hot noodlturkish piruhies to wilt.

3. Toss noodles with garlic, olive oil, lemon, basil, capers, salt and pepper. Divide and serve topped with salmon, tomatoes, and shredded parmesan if desired.

Beet Fettuccine – V

A unique dish with a funky appearance, the deep flavour of beet fettuccine blends well with *Olive Oil and Balsamic Sauce* and salty feta cheese.

Serves 2-4

1 batch *Beet Pasta Dough* cut into fettuccine noodles

1 tsp olive oil

Salt

3 Tbsp *Olive Oil and Balsamic Sauce*

¼ feta

½ c fresh chopped parsley

¼ c roughly chopped cashews

1. Bring a medium-sized pot of water to a boil. Add olive oil and sprinkle with salt. Boil noodles 1-3 minutes, until soft. Drain, toss with sauce and feta or goat cheese. Garnish with parsley and cashews.

Vegan Lasagna

Replacing the traditional ground meat filling with quinoa and veggies makes for a protein packed healthy lasagna. Choose a pasta dough option and cut it to create wide lasagna noodles. Feel free to experiment with unusual pasta dough options, like *Green Spinach Dough, Beet Pasta Dough,* or even *Chocolate Pasta Dough*!

Makes one 9x9" baking dish

1 batch *Basic Pasta Dough* of choice (or pre-packaged gluten free lasagna noodles)

Sweet rice flour for dusting

1½ c gluten free vegetable stock

¾ c uncooked quinoa, rinsed and drained in a fine mesh sieve

½ c finely diced tomato

½ c finely chopped onion

1 tsp dried oregano

1 carrot, peeled and finely diced

1 c dairy-free shredded cheese

Tomato Sauce

Approximately 2 c chopped tomatoes or 1 - 15oz can tomato purée

1 clove garlic

1 tsp dried basil

1 tsp dried parsley

1 Tbsp brown sugar

¼ tsp salt

¼ tsp pepper

1. Cut pasta dough into quarters. Remove one piece, covering the rest with a damp towel. Sprinkle a flat surface with sweet rice flour. Roll out dough paper thin, following the technique described for *Rolling Fettuccine and Lasagna*. Slice noodles into strips approximately 9" long and 2¼" wide. Repeat with remaining dough to create twelve lasagna noodles. Drop into a pot of boiling water and cook until the noodles float, then cook another 1-2 minutes. Drain and set aside.

2. In a medium-sized pot, bring stock, quinoa, tomato, onion, oregano, and carrot to a boil. Cover, reduce heat to simmer and cook for 20-25 minutes, until all liquid is absorbed. Remove from heat.

3. In a blender or food processor, blend tomatoes, garlic, basil, parsley, honey, salt and pepper until smooth.

4. Spread roughly ⅓ of the sauce over the bottom of a 9x9" baking pan. Lay four strips of noodles over the sauce. Spoon ½ of the quinoa mix over noodles and top with another ⅓ of sauce. Lay out another four strips of noodles and spoon remaining quinoa mix over strips. Cover with remaining noodles, sauce, and shredded cheese.

5. Bake lasagna 30 minutes at 350F, or until sauce is bubbling and cheese is melted.

Chapter 8: Beginnings and Endings - Breakfast and Dessert Pasta

Believe it or not, pasta can be had any time of day, breakfast and dessert included. In this chapter you'll find breakfast soup, pasta and eggs, dumplings, dessert pierogis, medieval-style ravioli, and more!

Shown below: Chocolate Fettuccine with whipped cream and cranberries

Chinese Breakfast Soup - V
Leftover Pasta and Egg Skillet
Red Bean Paste Filling - V
Pumpkin Pie Filling
Chocolate Ganache Filling - V

Glutinous/Sticky Rice Dumplings (Tang Yuan) in Ginger Syrup - V
Chocolate Pasta Dough - V
Cranberry Orange Filling - V
Ravioli Bianchi (White Ravioli)

Chinese Breakfast Soup – V

A comforting way to start a cool day, this breakfast soup is healthy, warming, and filling. It's also quick and easy to make, and is a good way to use up leftover meat or greens.

Serves 4

1 Tbsp olive oil

1 tsp freshly minced ginger

4 c gluten free chicken or vegetable stock

1 carrot, peeled and thinly sliced on an angle

4 oz vermicelli or bean thread noodles

1 egg, beaten (optional)

1 c kale or bok choy leaves, roughly chopped

Leftover cooked meat, thinly sliced or in small cubes (optional)

1 Tbsp gluten free soy sauce, or Coconut Aminos (for a gluten and soy free option)

1 Tbsp rice vinegar

¼ tsp salt

Garnish with chopped green onion and cilantro

1. In a medium-sized pot over medium-low heat, sauté ginger in olive oil 1 minutes. Add stock, carrot, and noodles and bring to a boil. Drizzle beaten egg into pot. Reduce to simmer and cook until noodles are softened, approximately 10 minutes.

2. Add kale or bok choy, meat, gluten free soy sauce, rice vinegar, and salt. Simmer 1-3 minutes to soften greens. Remove from heat and serve garnished with green onions and cilantro.

Leftover Pasta and Eggs Skillet

This pasta skillet is a wonderful, healthy way to use up pasta and veggie scraps from the night before. Serve for breakfast or brunch.

Serves 4

½ c dry fettuccine broken in pieces, OR elbow OR spiral pasta, OR 1 c *cooked* pasta

1 Tbsp oil for sautéing

2 Tbsp finely diced onion

2 c loosely packed chopped Swiss chard or spinach greens

4 eggs, scrambled

¼ c milk (cow, rice, or almond milk)

½ tsp dried dill OR 2 Tbsp fresh chopped dill, parsley, or cilantro + extra for garnish

¼ tsp salt

Pinch of pepper

Optional:
Finely diced red and green peppers
Grated parmesan or cheddar cheese
Finely diced sausage

1. If using uncooked pasta, cook pasta according to package directions. Drain.

2. In a medium-sized skillet, sauté onion in oil over medium heat 5-7 minutes, until translucent and just beginning to crisp.

3. Remove onions to a large bowl with pasta and all remaining ingredients, mix to combine.

4. Add extra oil to skillet if needed, heat on medium heat, and pour all ingredients into the skillet. Distribute evenly. Cover with a lid and cook 5-7 minutes, until sides start to take on a solid, cooked appearance. Run a spatula around edges and under noodles to loosen. Flip by either: placing a large plate over the skillet, flipping the skillet over onto the plate and then sliding it back onto the skillet, or place another oiled skillet of the same size over the top, flip and continue cooking in the new skillet. Cook another 3-6 minutes until eggs are cooked through.

Serve with chopped fresh herbs and parmesan.

Red Bean Paste Filling - V

Red bean paste is a common filling in various Asian countries for buns, dumplings, and even in soup. Red bean paste can be found ready-made in most Asian stores, but it is easy to make at home, just don't forget to soak the beans overnight before cooking. Home-cooking also allows you to adjust the sweetness of the paste to your liking. This is a great filling for *Steamed Dumpling Buns,* or *Glutinous/ Sticky Rice Dumplings.*

Makes approximately 1 ½ cups

½ c dried red adzuki beans

¼ c sugar + more if desired

1. Rinse beans and pick out any discolored ones and stones. In a bowl, cover beans with water and soak overnight, or about 8 hours.

2. Drain beans and cover again with water in a medium-sized pot. Bring water to a boil, reduce heat, and simmer 1 – 1 ½ hrs, until beans are soft.

3. Drain beans, reserving 2 Tbsp liquid. In a food processor or with a fork, mash or purée beans with reserved liquid until smooth. Stir in sugar. Return beans to pot.

4. Heat beans over low heat to reduce moisture and fry 3-5 minutes, stirring and pressing with a wooden spoon until beans form a paste.

Paste can be stored in a sealed container in the fridge for up to 1 week.

Pumpkin Pie Filling

It doesn't get much better than pumpkin pie wrapped up in pasta dough. A variation of the *Basic Gluten Free Pasta Dough* works great for making pumpkin pie ravioli or pierogi, while *Pumpkin Pie Pasta Dough* really makes this recipe pop. Top with whipped cream, sprinkle with powdered sugar, or a pinch of cinnamon mixed with brown sugar.

Makes 1 ½ cups

¾ c pumpkin purée

3 Tbsp brown sugar

1 egg

2 Tbsp heavy cream

¼ tsp vanilla

¾ tsp cinnamon

¼ tsp ground ginger

¼ tsp ground nutmeg

¼ tsp salt

1. In a medium-sized bowl, whisk together all ingredients. Scoop ½ - ¾ tsp filling onto dough, cut as desired to make ravioli or pierogi shapes, following directions for *Making Ravioli* or *Pierogi Dough and Shaping.*

Chocolate Ganache Filling - V

A decadent dessert filling for either chocolate or plain pierogi and ravioli, this ganache is sure to impress. Rich and not overly sweet, it will melt in your mouth. Serve plain, sprinkled with sugar, drizzled with chocolate, or topped with whipped cream. *Shown below with Chocolate Pasta Dough.*

Makes enough for 35-40 ravioli

---

4 oz dark chocolate
(i.e. 1 - 4 oz or 100g bar of dark chocolate or dairy-free chocolate)

½ c heavy cream or milk of choice
(i.e. cow, coconut, rice, or almond milk)

1. Chop chocolate into small chunks. Place in a medium-sized bowl.

2. In a heavy-bottomed pot, heat cream over medium-high heat, stirring frequently, until foaming and almost boiling. Do not burn or scald the cream. Pour over chocolate and whisk until chocolate melts evenly into cream. Refrigerate until thick and spreadable. Scoop ½ - 1 tsp spoonful onto pasta dough, following directions for making ravioli or pierogi.

Glutinous/Sticky Rice Dumplings (Tang Yuan) in Ginger Syrup - V

Despite the title, these dumplings *are* gluten free. They get their name from their glutinous texture, courtesy of glutinous rice flour, which is really made with sweet rice and no gluten at all. Sweet rice flour, or glutinous rice flour, creates a sticky paste when mixed with water. These soft, chewy dumplings are a tradition in China and parts of East Asia during the Dongzhi Festival to celebrate the winter solstice, as well as Yuanxiao, or the Lantern Festival, although they are also eaten year round. They are made as plain, small balls or filled with either a savory or sweet paste, like *Red Bean Paste*, black sesame seed paste, or mashed purple yam mixed with sugar, and served in sweet syrup (like the ginger syrup in this recipe) or a savory broth. Sometimes they are also brightly colored with a few drops of food coloring.

Makes approximately 35 balls

½ - 1 cup filling of choice (i.e. *Red Bean Paste*)

Rice Dumplings

2 c glutinous/sweet rice flour

1/2 Tbsp caster or super fine sugar (optional)

1 c water

Ginger Syrup

3 cups water

2" piece of ginger, peeled and thinly sliced

1 large ball of rock sugar or ½ c brown sugar

To make syrup: In a medium-sized pot, bring water, ginger, and sugar to a boil. Reduce to a simmer and stir until sugar is dissolved. Remove from heat and chill.

Prepare a large bowl of ice water.

1. In a bowl, mix flour and sugar. Add water and mix until a smooth paste is formed that is no longer sticky. Divide dough into quarters. Remove one quarter, covering remaining dough with a clean tea towel or paper towel. Roll each quarter into 8-10 balls.

2. Flatten each ball into a disc, and scoop a small amount of filling onto center.

3. Fold the edges up and press to seal. Gently roll into a smooth ball between palms of hands and set aside.

4. Bring a pot of water to a boil. Drop dumplings into boiling water and cook until they float. Boil one more minute, then remove with a slotted spoon and drop into the bowl of ice water to stop the cooking process. Once cooled, remove balls to the ginger syrup and serve chilled or at room temperature.

Chocolate Pasta Dough - V

A fun way to impress dinner guests, chocolate pasta dough can be used to make fettuccine noodles served with whipped cream, or stuffed with sweet fruit for pierogi, or filled with *Chocolate Ganache* to make dessert ravioli.

Serves 4 dessert portions or makes 30-40 ravioli or pierogi

- ½ c white rice flour or sorghum flour
- ¼ c cocoa powder
- ¼ c tapioca starch
- ¼ c sweet rice flour
- ¾ tsp xanthan gum or guar gum
- ⅛ tsp salt
- ½ Tbsp sugar
- ½ tsp vanilla extract
- 1 egg (or 1 Tbsp ground flax mixed with 3 Tbsp water)
- 1 Tbsp olive oil
- Water as needed (2-4 Tbsp)

1. Sift together sorghum flour, cocoa powder, starch, gum, salt, and sugar in a large bowl. Create a well in the center of the mix.

2. Place the egg or flax mixture in the center of the well, along with olive oil and 2 Tbsp of water. Whisk wet ingredients together with a fork, then blend in dry ingredients, adding in water by the spoonful as needed until dough forms a ball. Dough should be smooth, but not overly sticky. If too sticky, knead in a small amount of sweet rice flour when rolling out.

3. Cover bowl with a clean, damp tea towel until ready for use. Dough can be refrigerated up to 24 hours before use, no longer.

Cranberry Orange Filling - V

In Poland and other parts of Eastern Europe pierogi are filled with jams and fruit compotes for sweet desserts. This cranberry-orange filling is a sweet and slightly tart way to end a meal. Sweet fruit pierogi are usually served with applesauce, sugar and cinnamon, sour cream, yogurt, or whipped cream.

Makes enough for 30-40 pierogi

6 oz washed fresh cranberries (approximately 2 cups)
½ c sugar free orange juice
½ c sugar
¼ tsp salt

1. Add all ingredients to a medium-sized sauce pot. Heat over medium-high heat and cook until cranberries begin to pop open and release their pulp (about 10 minutes). Stir frequently until sauce is thickened. Watch out for hot splashes of cranberry. Remove from heat and allow to cool and gel before scooping onto pierogi dough in 1 tsp increments.

Ravioli Bianchi (White Ravioli)

As mentioned in the recipe for *Ravioli Nudi*, in medieval Italy "ravioli" didn't always mean stuffing wrapped in dough. In 1326, Sozzo Bandinelli's son was to be knighted. In honour of this week-long celebration, friends of the house sent dozens of peacocks and pheasants, huge pies, and game. Wine, meat, and bread were distributed to the local convents.[vi]

But it was a ravioli bianchi similar to this one that was served as a first course at a banquet on Christmas Day in honour of the occasion.[vii] These white ravioli are also known as *ravioli nudi* (nude ravioli), or sugar dumplings, for their slight sweetness. Like Sozzo Bandinelli, you may serve them as an appetizer, although contemporary palates might find them more suitable as a light dessert. Each one is a small bite full that melts in the mouth.

Makes approximately 10-12 ravioli balls

2 cups shredded mild white cheese (such as mozzarella, bocconcini, or farmer's cheese)

¾ Tbsp butter, softened

1 Tbsp sugar

¼ tsp ground ginger

¼ tsp ground cinnamon, divided

Pinch salt

1 egg white, lightly beaten

White rice flour for dredging

<u>For topping</u>

1 Tbsp sugar

¼ tsp cinnamon

1. In a food processor, mash cheese, butter, sugar, ginger, cinnamon, and salt until smooth. Work in egg white. Chill 15 minutes.

2. Put approximately ¼ - ½ cup of rice flour in a shallow bowl. Shape 1 Tbsp of cheese mix into a ball, dredge through flour and set aside.

3. Bring a medium-sized pot of water to a simmer. Gently drop the cheese balls into pot. When balls begin to float, remove from water with a skimmer or slotted spoon and drain well.

4. Mix sugar and cinnamon topping. Sprinkle balls with topping and serve warm or cold.

To freeze: Place raw, uncooked ravioli balls on a tray lined with waxed paper in freezer for ½ hour. Keep in a sealed container up to one month. To cook, remove from freezer and let defrost 15 minutes. Place in simmering water and cook as for fresh ravioli balls.

Endnotes

[i] Silvano Serventi and Françoise Sabban, trans. Antony Shugaar, *Pasta: The Story of a Universal Food,* New York: Columbia University Press, 2002, xvii.

[ii] John Roach, "4,000-Year-Old Noodles Found in China," *National Geographic News,* October 12, 2005. Available at http://news.nationalgeographic.com/news/2005/10/1012_051012_chinese_noodles_2.html

[iii] Odile Redon, Françoise Sabban, and Silvano Serventi, trans. Edward Schneider, *The Medieval Kitchen: Recipes from France and Italy,* Chicago: The University of Chicago Press, 2002, 62.

[iv] Robert and Maria Strybel, *Polish Heritage Cookery*, New York: Hippocrene Books, 2005, 456.

[v] Serventi, 26

[vi] J. Addington Symonds, "Folgore da San Gemignano," edited by John Morley, *The Fortnightly Review*, Volume XXIX, New Series, January 1 to June 1, 1881. London: Chapman and Hall, Limited, 364

[vii] Redon, 62.

Index

A
5 Minute Tomato Sauce, 63
Asian Dipping Sauce, 63
Asian Ground Meat Filling, 56
Asian Shrimp Filling, 56
Asian Veggie Filling, 57

B
Balsamic Browned Butter Sauce, 61
Basil Kale Pesto / Pistou, 60
Browned Butter Sage Sauce, 62
Butter and Poppy Seed Sauce, 66

C
Chinese Breakfast Soup, 79
Chocolate Ganache Filling, 82
Chocolate Pasta Dough, 85
Chow Fun, 74
Cranberry Orange Filling, 87

D
Dill and Feta Filling, 52

F
Fettuccine
    Beet Fettuccine, 76
    Chocolate Fettuccine, 78
    Raw Zucchini Fettuccine, 37
    Rolling Fettuccine, 13
    To freeze fettuccine, 14

G
Glutinous/Sticky Rice Dumplings (Tang Yuan) in Ginger Syrup, 83
Gnocchi
    Festival Squash Gnocchi, 30
    Gnocchi, 28
Ground Turkey Filling, 55

K
Kopytka, 32

L
Lasagna
    Rolling Lasagna, 13
    To freeze lasagna, 14
    Vegan Lasagna, 77
Leftover Pasta and Eggs Skillet, 80
Lemon Salmon Pasta, 75

M
Mediterranean Artichoke and Spinach Filling, 58
Mock Couscous, 38
Mock Moroccan Couscous Tagine, 69

O
Olive Oil and Balsamic Vinegar Sauce, 61
Orzo
    Hand-cut Orzo, 22
    Orzo and Chickpea Soup, 72

P
Pasta Dough
    Basic Pasta Dough, 18
    Beet Pasta Dough, 24
    Egg-Free or Vegan Pasta Dough, 18
    Green Spinach Dough, 18
    Millet Flour Pasta Dough - vegan & gum-free, 19
    Pumpkin Pie Dough, 25
    Red Tomato Dough, 18
    Sorghum Flour Dough, 18
    White Rice Flour Dough, 18
Pierogi Dough and Shaping, 40
Polish Cabbage and Mushroom Filling, 58
Potato and Onion Filling, 54
Pumpkin Pie Filling, 81

R

Ravioli
- How to make ravioli, 14
- Ravioli Bianchi (white ravioli), 88
- Ravioli Nudi (nude ravioli), 34

Raw Zucchini Spaghetti, 37
Red Bean Paste Filling, 81
Red Wine Tomato Sauce, 62
Ricotta and Spinach, 52
Ricotta and Spinach Filling, 52

S

Spaetzle, 23
Spaghetti Squash Pasta, 36
Squash and Spinach Filling, 53
Steamed Dumpling Buns (Bao / Baozi), 46
Steamed Rice Noodles, 20
Steaming
- How to Make a Steamer, 12
- Steamed Dumpling Buns (Bao / Baozi), 46

Steamed Rice Noodles (Ho Fun), 20
Sweet Potato Maple Filling, 54
Sweet Potato Noodles, 37

T

Tomato Cream Sauce, 63
Tortellini
- Spinach Tortellini Soup, 70
- Tri-Color Tortellini, 42

Turkish Piruhi, 49

V

Vegan Gravy, 64

W

White Cream Sauce, 66
Won Tons
- Making won tons, 45
- Won Ton Soup, 68

Thank you for choosing

Recipes for Unusual Gluten-Free Pasta:

Pierogis, Dumplings, Desserts and More!

If you enjoyed this book, please consider writing a review on Goodreads.com, Amazon.com or .ca, or other online locations to help others find it. For more by Danielle S. LeBlanc, check out *Living with Oral Allergy Syndrome: A Gluten and Meat-Free Cookbook for Soy, Wheat, Fresh Fruit and Vegetable Allergies*.

For free recipes, updates, articles, and more information on going gluten free or living with food allergies, follow Danielle S. LeBlanc and her blog **www.poorandglutenfree.blogspot.com**.

Find Danielle on Google + under:
Poor and Gluten Free

Follow Poor and Gluten Free on Facebook at:
Poor and Gluten Free (Gluten Free on a Budget)

Or on Twitter:
Poor and Gluten Free @GlutenFreeCheap

Find Danielle's recipe collections and DIY projects on Pinterest at:
http://www.pinterest.com/glutenfreecheap/